RECOGNIZING BRAIN
DYSFUNCTION:
A GUIDE FOR MENTAL
HEALTH PROFESSIONALS

RECOGNIZING BRAIN DYSFUNCTION: A GUIDE FOR MENTAL HEALTH PROFESSIONALS

Cooper B. Holmes
Emporia State University

Clinical Psychology Publishing Co., Inc.
4 Conant Square
Brandon, Vermont 05733

Library of Congress Cataloging-in-Publication Data

Holmes, Cooper B.
   Recognizing brain dysfunction : a guide for mental health professionals
/ Cooper B. Holmes.
      p.   cm.
   Includes bibliographical references and index.
   ISBN 0-88422-116-4 (pbk.) : $15.95
   1. Brain — Diseases — Psychological aspects. 2. Psychological
manifestations of general diseases. I. Title.
RC455.4.B5H65   1992
616.8'01'9--dc20   91-75520
                                            CIP

Library of Congress Catalog Card Number: 91-75520
ISBN: 0-88422-116-4

 4 Conant Square
Brandon, Vermont 05733

Printed in the United States of America.

Cover design by Sue Thomas.

This book is dedicated to Dee, Brenda, Katrina, Debbie, Lisa, Ashley, Andrew, and Brandon.

CONTENTS

ACKNOWLEDGMENTS

I must acknowledge Michael E. Howard, Ph.D., for the exceptional training he provided me in neuropsychology. I must thank Dr. Stephen F. Davis, Chairperson of the Division of Psychology and Special Education, Emporia State University, for his support. I owe special thanks to Gerald B. Fuller, Ph.D., President, Clinical Psychology Publishing Company, and to two anonymous reviewers whose comments resulted in a greatly improved manuscript.

1 INTRODUCTION

Consider the last 100 patients with whom you or your mental health facility had contact. Depending on which study you read, and the particular diagnosis involved, there is a high probability that some of those patients were suffering from a *serious* physical illness that either directly caused or significantly contributed to the presenting psychiatric condition. There is a surprisingly large chance that most of those clients were not aware of the illness. In better than 80% of the cases, the client's mental health worker will not have been aware of the physical problem. Even more disconcerting, there is a fairly good chance that the person's physician failed to detect the problem. Some of those last 100 clients, then, were physically ill but were diagnosed and treated as psychological cases. In fact, those people needed the attention of a physician. In Chapter 2, I will present the evidence that supports these rather remarkable claims. The evidence is compelling.

PURPOSE OF THIS BOOK

The purpose of this book is to alert mental health professionals to the possibility of misdiagnosing a physical problem as a psychiatric one, and to provide guidelines to help tell who is and is not likely to be suffering a brain disorder that is presenting with psychiatric symptoms. At the outset, let me note that this book will be focusing on brain dysfunction rather than on other forms of physical disease that either cause or contribute to a psychiatric diagnosis.

The focus in this book will be on those problems in which the brain is the primary affected organ. From time to time, though, it will be impossible to avoid discussing other illnesses. Take, for example, diabetes mellitus. Although this is not a brain disorder per se, it is a commonly overlooked illness in mental health settings. It is only one of many medical disorders that create definite psychiatric symptoms, yet are frequently not diagnosed prior to the client seeking psychiatric help (e.g., Koranyi, 1979).

THE ROLE OF PSYCHOLOGICAL THEORIES

Shifting toward a biological emphasis does not mean discrediting psychological theories or influences in mental health problems. No one seriously believes the human brain is programmed to produce the details of what people will be at age 15, 40, or 70. The brain is influenced by experience, not only in the physical sense, but in the psychological sense. The details of our lives depend greatly on the experiences to which we have been exposed. Traditional psychological theories are needed to help explain the influence of these environmental events. However, in some cases, psychological explanations are misleading. In all cases, understanding of both the environmental influences and the brain processes that store and relate them can only serve to enhance our understanding of people and our ability to help them.

In other words, use of psychological theories must be accompanied by knowledge of how the brain operates. Given that we are just on the frontiers of understanding the brain, the future holds great promise for an eventual integration of the psychological and biological emphases in explaining and treating mental problems.

TERMINOLOGY TO BE USED IN THIS BOOK

Throughout this book, various terms will be used to discuss the physical and psychological aspects of the screening process. Some writers make what seem to be unnecessarily fine distinctions between mental health terms (e.g., a psychological problem compared to an emotional problem compared to a mental problem). I have worked in the mental health field long enough to know that most of us do not make such distinctions; therefore, they will not be made in this book.

Problems considered to be of a purely psychological nature will be described as *psychogenic, psychological, psychiatric, mental, emotional,* or *functional.* These terms will be used interchangeably and should not be interpreted as reflecting subtle theoretical or professional differences.

In discussing a physical problem, several terms will be employed: *biological, physical, physiological, organic, medical, brain,* or *neurological.* These all refer to physical aspects of the person and, also, should not be interpreted as reflecting any particular theoretical or professional viewpoint.

When referring to a brain that is not functioning normally, the terms *impaired, dysfunction, damaged, disorder,* or *injured* will be used interchangeably (realizing that the term *injured* is being used rather broadly here). In later parts of this book, especially in Chapter 2, the terms brain *lesion* or *insult* will be used. These require explanation. The terms *lesion* and *insult* refer to *any* type of brain problem. Thus, they may refer to a tumor, gunshot wound, stroke, closed head injury, physical deterioration, or hematoma (a pool of blood, usually a blood clot).

The terms *mental health worker* or *mental health professional* will be used to describe anyone who works in the mental health field. Thus, the terms refer to anyone who provides mental health services, irrespective of professional identity, degree of training, or services provided.

When I began my study of neuropsychology, I had a strictly clinical and academic background. I recall how difficult my first readings were, primarily because of the scientific/medical terminology. Unless such terminology is absolutely necessary, I will avoid it in this book.

HOW MUCH KNOWLEDGE OF THE BRAIN IS NEEDED

No special knowledge of the brain and how it functions is necessary to be able to read this book and implement its suggestions. The emphasis of this book is on the screening process, not on training in neuroanatomy and neuropsychology. The only assumption made about the reader is that he or she is a mental health professional, which, in turn, implies familiarity with psychiatric diagnoses.

Because no special knowledge of the brain and how it functions is required to be able to use this book, you will note the absence of a section or chapter on the brain itself. There are two main reasons for this. First, it is simply not necessary to the purpose of this book. Second, if a section on the brain were included, it is likely you would feel compelled to study and perhaps memorize the material, and that would distract from the primary purpose of the book.

How much you ultimately need to know about brain functioning depends on your specific role, the types of referrals you or your agency receive, and the focus of your agency. If you want to know more about the brain and how it functions, there are many excellent introductory books on the topic. I certainly encourage you to read more about this if you have an interest. In Chapter 9 I present a suggested reading plan to help develop greater understanding of the brain.

HOW THE BRAIN PRODUCES PSYCHIATRIC SYMPTOMS

Although it is not necessary to understand brain anatomy and specific brain functions for the purpose of this book, it is useful to understand how brain problems produce psychiatric symptoms. Understanding this begins with the old mind/body argument that was so prevalent in psychology in the early part of this century (which, incidentally, is re-emerging today). If you are a *dualist,* you believe the mind and body are two separate entities; therefore, clear distinctions can be drawn between psychiatric and physical problems. If you are a *monist,* you believe the mind and body are one; therefore it is not possible to separate the mental from the physical. Although there are intermediate positions on this matter, as this is not a book about the history of psychology, I will simply note that the prevalent view among those who work with brain problems is a monist one. It follows, then, that when something goes physically wrong with the brain there will be some kind of mental manifestation. In some cases the mental manifestation will be obvious, as in delirium. In other cases the manifestation may be very subtle, as in slight changes in personality. It is these manifestations, both the obvious and the subtle, that are assessed when doing a neuropsychological examination.

Brain Structure

The brain is a physical organ with the consistency of gelatin. It is encased in a hard, unyielding skull. There are billions of neurons that communicate with each other to form transmission pathways for nerve impulses. These connecting pathways are incredibly fragile. The brain operates on a chemical/electrical basis, within the finest limits of tolerance. An imbalance of this delicate system will affect its performance.

Brain Systems

It is best to consider the brain as consisting of many areas that act in correspondence with each other to form systems (Luria, 1973). These systems are responsible for our thoughts and actions. For example, although we often hear of a "speech center" in the left hemisphere (for most people), this is only partially correct. The production of speech involves a number of areas in the brain, front and back, left and right, and, of course, all the connecting fibers that bring the system together. Given these points, it is readily apparent that there are numerous ways for the brain to malfunction. The following discussion presents the conditions that produce brain dysfunction.

Injury

Injuries that break through the skull, such as gunshot, are called penetrating injuries. The force of the blow as well as the tissue destruction in the path of the object create damage. Injuries that do not break the skull are called closed head injuries; for example, those resulting from a fall, a car wreck, or a child being violently shaken by a parent.

In a closed head injury the brain is shaken and twisted around the brain stem, which tears and separates connecting fibers (a process called axonal shearing) and may damage blood vessels, resulting in diffuse damage. Also, the brain is thrown against the skull. If the closed head injury involves a blow to the head (e.g., hitting the windshield or being hit by an object), damage at the point of impact is called the coup injury. However, damage is also likely to occur on the side of the brain opposite the point of impact, as the brain is thrown against the skull. This is called contrecoup injury. This is a very important point because a person who, for example, receives a blow to the left side of the head may well show symptoms of right-side damage because of contrecoup effects.

It is safe to say that in most closed head injuries there will be frontal damage, regardless of where the impact occurs (because the front of the brain rests in an area of the skull with bony ridges against which the brain hits). Hematomas (blood clots) are possible following an injury and may occur immediately or may not become apparent for weeks or months postinjury.

Noninjury Lesions

Here I am referring to such problems as tumors, strokes (blockages of blood supply), blockages of the flow of cerebral spinal fluid, or physical deterioration of parts of the brain. The symptoms the client shows are produced either by tissue destruction or by pressure exerted on or within the brain. For example, consider what happens when a tumor grows anywhere inside the cranial space. Because the skull cannot expand, cranial space is limited. As the tumor grows, it takes up more and more of the space that is supposed to be reserved for the brain (that is why a tumor, among other conditions, is called a space-occupying lesion). In the process, the brain is increasingly compressed, thus affecting its ability to function.

Oxygen and Glucose Deficiency

The brain operates within very small limits of tolerance. It cannot continue functioning efficiently if there is any more than the briefest interruption of oxygen and glucose supplies. Tissue destruction occurs within a few minutes if the brain's supply of oxygen is cut off (e.g., from a near drowning or suffocation for any reason). Because the brain depends on glucose for its energy to operate, any problem in glucose supply will impair function (as in hypoglycemia—low blood sugar).

Biochemical Imbalance

You recognize this factor, of course, as the most widely offered explanation of psychotic disorders. The brain has a multitude of chemical agents that it uses to transmit impulses between neurons. Some of these agents stimulate transmission, some inhibit it. The chemical agents interact with each other to produce normal brain function. Any excess or deficiency of these agents will affect brain performance. Anything that affects the brain's ability to utilize these chemicals will affect performance as well. Illnesses may produce this kind of impairment, but so do other factors. For example, over-the-counter medications as well as prescription drugs affect brain functioning. Alcohol and other drugs affect the biochemistry of the brain; otherwise, how could they produce the effects so many people seek? Of course, hormonal imbalances can also affect the biochemistry of the brain.

Cumulative Effects

The more we have learned about the brain, the more we have realized that a series of minor injuries can combine to produce major brain impairment. Therefore, be aware that even though any one event was not sufficient to produce a client's symptoms, the cumulative effect is quite capable of doing so. By now I am sure you have surmised that various forms of brain impairments may overlap with each other, and you are correct. There is no reason to think that a person with one type of brain impairment could not have a second form of impairment; for example, having a closed head injury along with a medical condition that affects the supply of oxygen to the brain.

YOUR TASK IS BECOMING MORE COMPLEX

Before discussing the remainder of the book I should address a concern that may have already occurred to you: that having to learn all of this material and having to screen for possible brain problems is making your job considerably more complex and difficult. There is no way around this. Yes, knowledge of screening for brain problems is adding to your already considerable requirements to be a competent mental health professional. However, this is one matter that cannot be ignored. As the research in the next chapter will clearly show, some of the people seeking mental health care are actually in need of medical care, and their assumed psychiatric condition will be completely cured by their medical treatment alone (some will be greatly improved by medical treatment but will still need mental health counseling). Having to screen for brain impairments is an unavoidable part of being in the mental health profession. You must have this knowledge if you hope to avoid misdiagnosis. Of course, it is not always an easy task to tell who is or is not a potential candidate for medical treatment, but the difficulty of the task does not lessen its importance.

THE REMAINDER OF THE BOOK

The preceding pages have set the stage for the rest of this book. Chapter 2 presents a review of the research literature on the brain and psychiatric symptoms. There is a large body of research with a consistent message, but it can be summarized in a fairly succinct manner. After reading Chapter 2 you will have no doubt about the need for knowledge of screening. Chapter 3 addresses the special role of the mental health professional in the screening process. Chapter 4 begins the actual screening part of the book with discussion of perhaps the most important task of all: getting a detailed history of the person. In Chapter 5, I will present a number of the physical signs that should alert you to the possibility of brain problems. The physical signs presented in the chapter are those anyone can recognize, not signs that require a medical examination. Chapter 6 presents the psychological/cognitive signs that are common in brain problems and that can easily be mistaken as signs of psychiatric illness. Chapter 7 addresses the topic of using tests in screening for organicity. Chapter 8 discusses the referral process in the event you have reason to suspect a brain disorder. Chapter 9 presents a suggested program of reading for those of you who want to acquire greater understanding of the brain and neurodiagnostic procedures. A guided program of reading is presented, with a list of books that I have found most helpful in my own reading.

The guidelines presented in the remainder of this book are in most instances applicable to both children and adults. It will be obvious when a given factor is not appropriate for both groups. As is true of any type of assessment of children, in screening for organicity what is or is not within normal limits must take into account the child's present developmental level.

2 THE NEED: RESEARCH ON THE BRAIN AND PSYCHIATRIC SYMPTOMS

There is a large body of research on the topic of brain problems presenting with psychiatric symptoms. The literature admonishing psychiatrists to be alert for organic disorders dates back as far as 1894 (McIntyre & Romano, 1977). Although it is encouraging to realize that a large number of researchers have addressed this problem, it is somewhat disturbing that many mental health workers are unaware of the studies. The mistaken belief is that this is an interesting area for those with a biological emphasis, but it has little to do with the mental health center, psychiatric hospital, or private practice. It has *everything* to do with mental health practice, and the following studies must be carefully considered.

The list of references for this chapter contains over 100 entries. If this seems to be a large number, consider that the studies presented here deal principally with clients who had undiagnosed brain problems that were presenting with psychiatric symptoms. There is another even larger body of studies dealing with the psychiatric symptoms of *known* physical illnesses, including brain disorders. Clearly, the two areas of research overlap a great deal; however, I am focusing on the undiagnosed brain problem for two reasons. First, to try to review all the studies on psychiatric symptoms of known medical illnesses would easily constitute a book in itself. In fact, there are already a number of excellent books on this topic to which I will be referring. Several of these books are listed at the end of this chapter. Second, and perhaps most important, if the patient has a known medical illness, he or she is already in contact with the medical profession and does not need to be screened. This does not mean that the presence of a known illness guarantees recognition of psychiatric symptoms. To the contrary, the literature shows that significant numbers of medical patients suffer psychiatric symptoms that are misunderstood because the relationship with a medical condition is not recognized. Because the present book is concerned with screening for possible organicity, the focus of the following review is on undiagnosed organic conditions you are likely to encounter in your practice.

For the sake of clarity and organization, the following studies have been grouped into several categories. Such grouping is rather arbitrary in some cases, as the studies typically addressed a number of factors. For example, there is a section on general surveys and a section dealing with elderly clients. Some of the general surveys included older clients; thus, those studies could have fit either section. The studies are not duplicated in different sections; rather, all pertinent information is presented in whichever section the study appears.

I recognize that the sections to follow are not going to be exactly exciting reading, but bear with me. I have kept the data and details of the studies to a minimum to help make reading a less tedious task. Stick with it and by the time you have finished this chapter you will have no doubt that going through the research was well worth it. I encourage you to mark those studies that have special significance for you in light of the clients with whom you work and the setting in which you practice. I strongly encourage you to obtain those articles and read them in detail. There is a great deal more information in the articles than I can present in a brief review. I have emphasized certain key parts of the studies, but you may find some of the other details especially useful. For the most part, I have retained the original diagnostic terms that were used in the articles, even though they may seem outmoded by current diagnostic standards. I did this to avoid possible misrepresentation of the researchers' material. Throughout the following review, the term *psychiatric* will be used to describe conditions of a purely psychological (functional) nature. This simply reflects the fact that "psychiatric" was the term used in virtually every article.

GENERAL SURVEYS

In this section are the results of studies in which patients who sought or were in psychiatric treatment were examined for physical illnesses. As you will see, in a surprising number of cases those illnesses either directly caused or contributed to the psychiatric disturbance. Terms such as *client, patient, hospital,* or *clinic,* for example, will refer to psychiatric cases unless it is specifically stated otherwise. To avoid unnecessary repetition, I will note at the outset that when researchers considered patients to have serious medical disorders they meant exactly that. Throughout the research, the illnesses ranged from endocrine disturbances to heart conditions to cancer to brain tumors. In only a few instances were the medical conditions so unusual or occult that failure to diagnose them accurately might be expected.

Mainly Outpatients

Psychiatric patients have been shown to have a significantly greater number of physical diseases of all kinds (Eastwood & Trevelyan, 1972). Roessler and Greenfield (1961) found that among college students seeking psychiatric help, 11 of 13 illnesses were more common in the psychiatric group than among other students. A number of studies have assessed rates of physical illness and then estimated the number of cases in which the illness was causal or contributed to the psychiatric symptoms. A study of 910 outpatients (Muecke & Krueger, 1981) found 20 newly diagnosed medical problems, of which 32% were either causal or related to the psychiatric condition. A similar study found that of 99 physical examinations prior to mental health care, 45% revealed information that could affect the clinical course of treatment for the psychiatric problem (Mannino & Wylie, 1965). Barnes, Mason, Greer, and Ray (1983) found that among 147 chronic outpatients, 26% had some form of physical disease, 13% of which were diagnosed for the first time during the study. The researchers concluded that in less than 1% of the cases the medical problem caused the psychiatric symptoms.

In a study of 677 outpatients and 433 inpatients, Forsythe, Ilk, Bard, and Wolford (1977) found that 56% of the patients had a diagnosable medical illness and that 29% of the conditions were first diagnosed during the study. Hall, Popkin, DeVaul, Faillace, and Stickney (1978) studied 658 outpatients, finding that in 9.1% of the cases a medical problem was the direct cause of psychiatric symptoms. Further, they noted that the most frequent psychiatric diagnoses among the medically ill were psychosis, organic problems, depression, and some form of neurosis.

Koranyi presented two similar studies on medical illnesses presenting psychiatrically. In the first study (Koranyi, 1972), of 100 outpatients, 49 were found to have a significant physical disorder, whereas many of the remaining 51 had minor medical conditions. Of the 49 medically ill patients, 24 were newly diagnosed in the study and 10 more who had a known medical condition were found to have another, previously undiagnosed one. Ten of the 49 patients had a medical condition directly causing psychiatric symptoms, while in 23 cases the medical problem aggravated the psychiatric one. Perhaps the most disconcerting finding of this study was that previous medical services had diagnosed only two thirds of the illnesses, psychiatrists had diagnosed only one half of the medical problems, and social agencies had detected only 12.5% of their patients' medical conditions.

The second study by Koranyi (1979) involved a thorough medical examination of 2,090 patients at a psychiatric clinic. He found that 43% of the patients had one or more serious medical conditions and that 46% of these cases had *not* been diagnosed before coming to the clinic. Koranyi noted that medical diseases were correctly diagnosed in 68% of the referrals from physicians (i.e., they missed 32% of the cases). The medical problem was detected in 52% of the referrals from psychiatrists. Social agencies were aware of the patients' problems in 17% of the cases, which was only one percentage point higher than the number of patients who were themselves aware of the problems. Koranyi concluded that in 18% of the cases, the medical condition directly caused the psychiatric problem, and that in another 51% of the cases, the psychiatric condition was aggravated by the medical disease.

In 1977, Koranyi published an article on fatalities among psychiatric patients. Over a 3-year period, of 2,070 outpatients there were 28 deaths, 13 from natural causes. All of these 13 patients had been initially referred by physicians, yet 6 of the patients had an undetected major illness (e.g., cancer, hydrocephalus, heart condition).

Mainly Inpatients

A study of 133 day hospital patients found that half of them had a medical illness and that 30% of those illnesses were first diagnosed during the study (Burke, 1978). The Department of Health, Education and Welfare (1973) found that of 592,000 patients discharged from general hospital psychiatric units, 12% carried an OMD (organic mental disease) diagnosis. Of patients 65 years and older, the number of OMD diagnoses nearly tripled, to a rate of 34.6%. Eastwood (1975) studied patients between 40 and 64 years of age and found that half of them had some kind of medical disease. He also found that older patients were more likely to have medical illnesses and that the greater the degree of psychiatric disturbance, the greater the number of physical problems.

Among 1,259 inpatients, 18% had a medical problem (Eilenberg & Whatmore, 1961). In 7% of those patients, the medical illness directly caused the psychiatric symptoms. Herridge (1960) studied 209 consecutive hospital admissions, finding that 34 patients had a significant medical condition that was unrelated to the psychiatric picture. In 43 patients a physical condition (13 of which were neurological) contributed to the psychiatric disorder, whereas in 11 cases (5%) a physical illness was directly causal.

Johnson (1968), in a study of 250 consecutive inpatient admissions, discovered that 60% of the patients had abnormal physical findings. In 12% of the cases the physical disorder directly caused the psychiatric symptoms. Johnson noted that 80% of the illnesses had not been diagnosed by the patient's physician. Kellner (1966) followed 947 patients from a general medical practice for 2 years. He found that minor psychiatric symptoms were more common after a medical diagnosis than at any other time.

Comparing 272 psychiatric patients to a control group, Lovett Doust (1952) found a higher rate of medical illness among the psychiatric group. Maguire and Granville-Grossman (1968) found that 67 (33.5%) of 200 inpatients had a physical disease, of which 47 were considered serious. One third of the illnesses were previously undiagnosed. Phillips (1937) noted that of 164 inpatients, 68% had physical problems. Martin (1962, cited in Saravay & Koran, 1977) found that 2% of 7,500 psychiatric admissions were suffering from previously undiagnosed medical illnesses. In a 1-day survey, Romano (1970) found that 49 of 92 patients (53%) had what he called notable medical or surgical problems. Snaith and Jacobson (1965) studied 428 inpatients and found that 15% were physically ill, of which the physical problem was directly causal in 8% of the cases. Wynne-Davies (1965) found that 15 of 36 new inpatients (41.7%) had a medical condition that contributed to the psychiatric symptoms.

Weinberger (1984) noted that research indicates 2% to 10% of psychiatric cases have a diagnosis of structural brain impairment. This article offered some helpful guidelines as to when a CT scan should be ordered. Wingfield (1967, cited in Saravay & Koran, 1977) found that 3.5% of 285 patients referred by physicians actually suffered medical problems that were primarily responsible for the symptoms that led to the referral.

The medical conditions that were missed included disorders such as epilepsy and multiple sclerosis.

In a study of 175 inpatients, Marshall (1949) found 44% (77 patients) had a physical condition needing medical attention. Four illnesses (3%) were previously undiagnosed. Look at the four undiagnosed problems: tuberculosis, cancer, glioma (a type of brain tumor), and major epilepsy. For 39 patients (22% of the total) the physical illness contributed to the psychiatric one. Although no further information was offered, Sandifer (1977) noted that slightly over one third of the inpatients in his study had a definable physical problem. Seidman (1983) presented a comprehensive review of the literature on the neurological aspects of schizophrenia, concluding that research indicates a 20% to 35% rate of neurological impairments among patients diagnosed as schizophrenic.

In a rather unique study, Saravay and Koran (1977) noted that 4% of patients referred by physicians were actually medically ill. The unique part of the study was the authors' discussion of four *obvious* cases of organic disorder that the primary physician had decided was psychological in nature. Saravay and Koran analyzed reasons why the primary physician ignored the obvious physical signs.

Abrams and Taylor (1976) found that 9 of 55 catatonic patients were actually organically impaired. Gelenberg (1976) also addressed catatonic states and described a number of medical conditions that can create such symptoms (ranging from reaction to aspirin to brain damage).

Stokes, Nabarro, Rosenheim, and Dunkley (1954) found that 1 in every 100 patients referred to a psychiatric unit by a general practitioner had a physical illness requiring medical or surgical treatment. The medical conditions included brain tumors, meningitis, cancer and heart conditions. Although no number was given, some of these 100 patients died.

The last few studies in this section will be presented in a bit more detail than the previous studies. Certain of their specific findings are dramatic and help to emphasize the point of this review of the research.

Hall, Gardner, Stickney, LeCann, and Popkin (1980) examined a state hospital sample of 100 patients (76 of whom were clearly psychotic at the time of admission). Eighty percent of the patients had some form of medical condition, of which 34% were directly in need of attention. Forty-six percent of the patients had a previously undiagnosed medical problem that was causing or exacerbating the psychiatric one. Of this 46% of the patients, 28 (or 61% of this group) showed a rapid clearing of psychiatric symptoms when the medical problem was treated. Another 18 patients showed significant psychiatric improvement after medical treatment. It is interesting to note that the treatment for these "psychiatric" (quotation marks mine) disorders included both medicine and surgery.

In addition to an excellent review of the literature, Koran et al. (1989) presented a study of 509 patients from all areas of mental health services (e.g., inpatient, outpatient, day hospital, emergency). Overall, 39% of the patients had an active, significant medical disease, but specific rates varied according to the mental health setting. Two hundred patients had a total of 291 physical diseases. Of these 291 diseases, the mental health system had diagnosed 52.5%. Twenty-five percent of the medical illnesses were newly diagnosed during the study. In a suprising finding (surprising to me), 27% of the diseases were known to the patient but *not to the mental health system*. Koran et al. concluded that in 6% of the cases, the medical disease caused the psychiatric condition, whereas another 9% involved the medical problem exacerbating the psychiatric symptoms. Of the 78 neurological problems diagnosed in the study, the mental health system had correctly diagnosed 64% of them.

One of the tables in the Koran et al. (1989) article was most informative. It presented a summary of several other studies of medical illnesses with psychiatric presentation. From the data in the table, I calculated the following means. The mean of 12 studies was 40.67% for patients with a medical illness. A mean of 23.20% of the patients (from 10 studies) were previously undiagnosed. From nine studies, a mean of 19.55% of the patients had a medical illness that was either causal of or contributed to the psychiatric condition. Based on six studies, a mean of 3.67% of the patients had psychiatric symptoms that were directly caused by the medical condition. Figures such as these should be of concern to all practitioners in the mental health field.

Rossman (1969) studied 130 patients who were initially diagnosed as psychiatric but were later diagnosed as medical. The initial diagnoses ranged from behavioral disturbance to neurosis to schizophrenia. A very long list of medical diagnoses was uncovered, with CNS problems being common (e.g., a case of amyotrophic lateral sclerosis—Lou Gehrig's disease—and one glioblastoma multiforme—an especially dangerous form of brain tumor). After correct diagnosis and treatment, 48 patients (36.9%) were completely cured of their psychiatric condition, 45 (34.6%) were improved, and 5 (3.9%) were unimproved. Thirty-two (24.6%) of the 130 patients died.

In what I consider to be the most disturbing finding of all the studies, Rossman (1969) provided information on 12 of the 130 patients who had been given electroconvulsive therapy before their medical problem was correctly diagnosed. Using Rossman's diagnoses, 2 of the 12 were diagnosed schizophrenic (real diagnosis: brain tumor in both), 1 depression (brain tumor), 1 anorexia nervosa (epileptic equivalent), 1 postmenopausal depression (aortic aneurism—just imagine this person getting shock treatments), 1 psychoneurosis (brucellosis), 1 behavior disorder (seizure dysrhythmia), 1 neurosis (chronic pelvic inflammation), 1 depressive personality (drug intoxication), 2 anxiety neurosis (hyperthyroid), and 1 depressive state (hyperthyroid).

Mainly Emergency Patients

Although several of the previous articles involved emergency patients as part of their studies, three articles dealt specifically with this group. One study of 2,000 emergency psychiatric patients found that in 5% of the cases a physical illness directly caused the psychiatric condition (Carlson, Nayar, & Suh, 1981). Browning, Miller, and Tyson (1974) studied patients who had come for emergency room psychiatric treatment and found that over the next 6 months those patients had over double the usual hospital admission rate for medical reasons. In other words, perhaps the emergency psychiatric contact was actually an early indicator of some medical disorder. In a study of 100 psychiatric emergencies, Eastwood, Mindham, and Tennett (1970) found that 40% had a medical disease. In 16% of the cases the medical disease was first diagnosed during the study. Eastwood et al. concluded that in 1% of the cases the physical illness directly caused the psychiatric symptoms.

Discussions Only

Several articles did not present research results but did offer discussions on differentiating psychiatric from organic conditions. Cummings (1988) presented an excellent discussion of factors to help differentiate medical from purely psychological disorders. Hall, Gruzenski, and Popkin (1979) presented a good discussion of which physical problems are likely to present with psychiatric symptoms, whereas Hall and Popkin (1977) cautioned against *assuming* a psychological cause for psychiatric symptoms. Other studies that have addressed differentiating signs for organic and psychiatric disorders are Lipowski (1975) and Shulman (1977).

Conclusions

This concludes the section on general surveys. It is clear that it is not a rare occurrence for a person seeking psychiatric help to have a medical condition that is either causing or contributing to the symptom picture. Now is a good time to provide a quick summary of the research. To do this, I have tabulated the results of those studies from which relatively clear information could be obtained. I do not in any way profess this to be a thorough statistical analysis, but it is a way of bringing all of this information into some kind of focus. Nineteen studies reported that an average of 39.37% of the patients had a medical condition (the range was from 4% to 60%). Twelve studies reported that from 2% to 46% of the medical problems were diagnosed for the first time during the study (with a mean of 23.25%). In 13 studies it was reported that in a mean of 7% of the cases the physical problem directly *caused* the psychiatric symptoms (the range was from 1% to 18%). Seven studies reported that in a mean of 30.86% of the cases the physical condition contributed to the psychiatric condition (the range was from 9% to 51%).

To keep proper perspective on the situation, it is important to remember that a mean of 7% with a directly causal medical condition also indicates that a mean of 93% *did not* involve such a causal factor. Doing the same thing for the other figures clearly tells us not to panic and asssume that every client walking through the door has a serious medical condition that requires an immediate referral. The data do make it quite clear that we are going to have to do a better job than we have done in the past of detecting organic cases when they do present themselves.

STUDIES SPECIFICALLY INVOLVING BRAIN DISORDERS

In the previous section, studies dealing with general rates of undiagnosed medical illnesses presenting psychiatrically were examined. In those articles, all types of medical illnesses were covered. In this section, the studies deal only with neurological diagnoses as the medical condition. It is not always possible to avoid esoteric terminology in the following discussion, but it will be kept to a minimum. When terminology cannot be avoided, I will briefly explain the term. It is not critical that you have a precise understanding of what the terms mean. The articles' main points can be made without such detailed knowledge.

General Articles

Benson (1973) presented a discussion of the psychiatric disorders (e.g., schizophrenia) that may be confused with aphasia. Aphasia is a disturbance of language abilities due to brain impairment (Strub & Black, 1988). For a good discussion of psychiatric symptoms associated with focal lesions of the nervous system (remember, lesion refers to any kind of damage), read Benson and Geschwind (1975). Multiple sclerosis has been described as presenting a wide variety of psychiatric symptoms (Braceland & Griffin, 1950). Selzer and Sherwin (1978) cited figures indicating that 20% of first inpatient admissions are organic cases. Selzer and Sherwin also noted a tendency to diagnose general categories when more specific diagnoses could have been made. They found that 77 of 80 VA patients could have been given a more specific diagnosis than they had received.

In a study of 128 patients with a variety of brain tumors, Soniat (1951) found that 51.5% of the patients initially presented with psychiatric symptoms. Soniat further noted the relationship between temporal lobe dysfunction and an increased likelihood of hallucinations. Spudis, Rogers, and Stein (1977) offered points on the management of psychiatric patients with brain tumors. Also in relation to brain tumors, Remington and Rubert (1962) reported 34 cases of brain tumor patients who had originally been admitted to psychiatric hospitals with a diagnosis of psychosis. Twenty-four of the tumors were previously undiagnosed.

Tissenbaum, Harter, and Friedman (1951) studied 395 cases of neurological disorders and found that 53 of them (13.4%) carried an initial psychiatric diagnosis made from 1 to 8 years earlier (the mean was 4.5 years). These 53 patients were eventually given 65 psychiatric diagnoses over the years: 50 were for some form of neurosis (with conversion or hysteria being the most common), 8 were somatization diagnoses, 5 were psychopathic personality, and 2 were schizophrenia. The most commonly missed neurological disorder was Parkinson's disease (40% misdiagnosed as psychiatric), followed by multiple sclerosis (33.3% missed), expanding brain lesions (30.7%), herniated disk (17.2%), neuritis (6.5%), and epilepsy (5.7%). Ten other neurological problems were misdiagnosed, ranging from encephalitis (brain infection) to amyotrophic lateral sclerosis.

Several studies reported autopsy results. Cole (1978) reported postmortem results on 200 mental hospital patients. He found 27 (13.5%)

of the patients had a previously undiagnosed space-occupying mass (this usually refers to a tumor). Just imagine, 13.5% of the hospitalized patients had an undiagnosed brain tumor. Patton and Sheppard (1956) described the results of 2,161 autopsies at a large state hospital. They found 77 patients (3.6%) had 78 previously undiagnosed brain tumors. The article went into considerable detail about the types of tumors that were found, but that discussion is not necessary here. An especially important finding of the Patton and Sheppard study was that 12 of the 78 tumors were metastatic (had spread from some other part of the body: 5 from lungs, 4 from breasts, 2 from kidneys, and 1 from the uterus). These authors noted a high incidence of a type of tumor called meningioma, which is a tumor of the covering membranes of the brain— the meninges—and not a tumor in the brain itself.

Selecki (1965) also studied meningiomas and found that they were more common at autopsy in mental hospitals than in general hospitals (from 24.4% to 46.4% for mental hospitals, and 6% to 18% for general hospitals). Selecki went on to note that meningiomas were 4 times as common among psychiatric patients as general medical patients, that meningiomas were the most common form of tumor to produce psychiatric symptoms, and that meningiomas frequently produced *only* psychiatric symptoms. The article noted that the patients ranged from 1 to 13 years of psychiatric treatment *before* the tumor diagnosis.

In another study dealing with meningiomas, Wood, White, and Kernohan (1957) reported 100 meningiomas found incidentally at autopsy (from a total of 300 brain tumors). Age differences were found, in that asymptomatic meningiomas were most common in people in their 70s and 80s, whereas symptomatic tumors were more common in people in their 50s. I should note, however, that the ages of the people who died ranged from 25 to 97 years.

In an article published in 1980, Adams, Jergenson, Kassell, and Sahs reported that one quarter of patients with subarachnoid hemorrhages were initially misdiagnosed. A subarachnoid hemorrhage refers to bleeding between the arachnoid membrane and the pia mater, two of the meninges that surround the brain. In a recent study showing only slightly better results, Adams, Kassell, Boarini, and Kongable (1991) found that 56 of 286 (19.6%) cases of aneurysmal subarachnoid hemorrhage were initially misdiagnosed, with tension headache being the most frequent diagnosis (14 cases) and viral syndrome or "flu" second (11 cases).

Subcortical Lesions

A number of studies have addressed lesions in brain areas lying below the cortex. Alpers (1940) discussed the relationship of psychiatric symptoms to tumors in the hypothalamus (in the brain stem area). A wide range of psychiatric symptoms was reported among patients with tumors in the basal ganglia (Brenner, Friedman, & Merritt, 1947). The basal ganglia are involved in performing physical movements. Malamud (1967) reported 18 autopsies of patients who had originally been diagnosed psychiatric (10 schizophrenic, 4 depression, 3 neurotic, and 1 manic). All were found to have tumors of the limbic system (a group of brain areas involved in emotional reactions, among other functions).

Malamud (1967) went on to note that in previous, unpublished research, he had found that of 65 frontal tumors, 80% had psychiatric symptoms; of 53 temporal tumors, 75% had psychiatric symptoms; of 42 parietal tumors, 45% had psychiatric involvement; of 44 3rd-ventricle tumors (at the upper part of the brain stem), 90% had mental symptoms; and of 41 tumors of the posterior fossa (at the base of the brain at the back), 10% presented psychiatric symptoms.

Frontal Lesions

In 1971, Avery discussed seven cases of frontal lobe tumors presenting with psychiatric symptoms. Three patients were described as apathetic, one was depressed, one was euphoric, one was manic-like, and one had a weakness of the legs that was attributed to stress. Direkze, Bayliss, and Cutting (1971) pointed out the relationship between frontal lobe tumors and disturbances of mood, a point also made by Faust (1966). Reporting on three cases of frontal meningiomas, Hunter, Blackwood, and Bull (1968) noted the initial diagnoses were depression, dementia, and psychosis. It is interesting to note that the three patients had had the tumors for 3, 25, and 43 years prior to accurate diagnosis. Hunter, Blackwood, and Bull cited warnings dating back to 1903 about being too quick to diagnose psychiatric symptoms. According to Strauss and Keschner (1935), 90% of patients with frontal tumors present some degree of psychiatric manifestation.

Kanakaratnam and Direkze (1976) found that of 56 patients with frontal tumors, 26 (46%) initially presented psychiatrically (12 depression, 6 presenile dementia, 5 schizophrenia, 2 anxiety, and 1 inadequate personality). These authors made two statements that are worth quoting.

First, "Psychiatric symptoms associated with intracranial tumours may be subject to remissions, relapses, or may follow a chronic course much as with functional psychiatric illnesses" (p. 221). Also, "Meningiomas have the innate potential to remain masked during the lifespan of the patient" (p. 221).

Epilepsy

Among 1,073 persons diagnosed as epileptic, Bartlett (1957) found 8 schizophrenic and 3 mood disturbance diagnoses. Lawall (1976) discussed how various forms of epilepsy may be confused with psychiatric disorders. The psychiatric symptoms described in the Lawall article covered a wide range, from neurotic to psychotic. In a 10-year study of hospital admissions, Slater and Beard (1963) found 69 cases of epilepsy whose symptoms closely resembled schizophrenia.

Temporal Lobes

Malamud (1957, 1966) noted the relationship between temporal lobe tumors and psychiatric symptoms. Rodin, DeJong, Waggoner, and Bagchi (1957) described 6 cases of temporal lobe abnormalities who exhibited classic signs of schizophrenia. Keschner, Bender, and Strauss (1936) found that 94% of patients with temporal lobe tumors reported psychiatric symptoms. In 1958, Bingley reported his study of 253 patients with temporal lobe gliomas (a type of brain tumor) and 16 temporal lobe epilepsy cases with benign gliomas and noted a high rate of mental symptoms but no blatant psychosis among the patients.

In a study of temporal lobe epilepsy, Gibbs (1951) found that half the patients had psychiatric symptoms and that these symptoms were three times as common if the impairment was in the front part of the temporal lobes. Ervin, Epstein, and King (1955) studied 42 patients with EEG abnormalities in the temporal lobes. The researchers noted that 81% of the patients had been diagnosed schizophrenic, irrespective of whether or not there were seizures. Along the same line, Serafetinides and Falconer (1962) studied 100 cases of temporal lobe epilepsy and found that 15 had been diagnosed psychotic. Mulder and Daly (1952) found that among 100 patients with temporal lobe lesions, 24 initially presented psychiatrically, ranging from depression to anxiety to schizoid traits.

Conclusions

Reviewing this section on brain disorders leads to the inescapable conclusion that brain disorders, especially tumors, frequently present with psychiatric symptoms, with psychosis being a predominant diagnosis. One type of tumor, meningioma, was mentioned again and again, not only because of its frequency but because of its ability to remain undiagnosed while mimicking functional disorders.

STUDIES SPECIFICALLY DEALING WITH CHILDREN

When reading the literature on medical illness and psychiatric symptoms, a rather glaring deficiency stands out. There are few studies that deal with undiagnosed medical illnesses presenting psychiatrically among children and adolescents. Many of the studies presented in this section deal with children who had been head injured. Although the general purpose of this review is to focus on undiagnosed medical illnesses, much can be learned by recognizing the psychiatric symptoms that frequently accompany a head injury.

Head Injury

Rutter (1977) reviewed the literature on brain syndromes in children and presented conclusions about children 5–14 years of age. He noted that among the general population of children the rate for psychiatric disorders was 6.6%, that children with physical disabilities had an 11.5% rate, and that brain-injured children had a rate of 34.3%. Rutter concluded, "But, equally, studies have clearly shown the major importance of brain damage as a factor contributing in a substantial way to the genesis of child psychiatric disorder" (p. 19). In a later article, Rutter (1981) noted that adults and children are equally likely to develop psychiatric complications after a brain injury. Further, premorbidly active children are more likely than other children to develop psychiatric symptoms after an injury, a point also noted by Burton (1968).

At this point, before going on, it may occur to you that if children have a brain injury the situation will be under control and all necessary information will be known and properly addressed. This is not so. As I have noted elsewhere (Holmes, 1988), people can be brain injured and not know it. Also, many professionals do not connect psychiatric symptoms with a brain dysfunction even when the injury or illness is known.

Brink, Garrett, Hale, Woo-Sam, and Nickel (1970) noted that children 10 years of age or older who have sustained a severe brain injury are likely to show hyperactivity, short attention span, impulsivity, and aggressiveness. In contrast, severely injured children under the age of 10 years are more likely to show mood symptoms and poor judgment. According to Klonoff and Low (1974), boys are more prone than girls to postinjury irritability, whereas personality changes (a common effect of head injury) are equally likely for boys and girls. Rutter, Graham, and Yule (1970) reported that psychiatric symptoms are more likely if there is bilateral brain damage (both sides), if the child came from a disturbed home, or if the child had seizures or abnormal EEG results. The effects of coming from a disturbed home and the effects of epilepsy were reaffirmed in a later study (Shaffer, Chadwick, & Rutter, 1975). Two studies have shown a relationship between premorbid low IQ, poor reading ability, and psychiatric symptoms following a head injury (Brown, Chadwick, Shaffer, Rutter, & Traub, 1981; Seidel, Chadwick, & Rutter, 1975).

Children and Adolescents in Psychiatric Care

Compared to an expected rate of neurological problems of 5% for adolescents in general, Hertzig and Birch (1968) found 34% of psychiatrically disturbed adolescents had some kind of neurological involvement. Further, only 6% of these adolescents had been diagnosed by the psychiatric staff as neurologically impaired. Tramontana, Sherrets, and Golden (1980) studied children and adolescents with psychiatric diagnoses and found that of those with normal neurological results, 60% had abnormal neuropsychological test results. Let me note that abnormal neuropsychological results do not necessarily indicate definite brain damage (e.g., schizophrenic patients routinely produce abnormal neuropsychological test results).

One of the most informative studies in this area was done by Ritvo, Ornitz, and Walter (1970). Although their study was concerned with EEG results, the following information is important to this review. The study involved 184 hospitalized children. Of the 33 children with a diagnosis of neurosis, 3 (9.1%) were definitely organic (had neurological signs), and another 10 (30.3%) were probably organic (history or medical results showed a CNS disturbance to be likely). Of 86 children diagnosed psychotic, 10 (11.6%) were definitely organic and 19 (22.1%) were probably organic. Of 7 psychophysiological diagnoses, none was definitely organic, whereas 2 (28.6%) were probably so. Of 58 children diagnosed as behavior disordered, 6 (10.3%) were definitely organic and 16 (25.5%) were probably organic. Combining all of these diagnoses, of the 184 children, 19 (10.3%) were definitely organic, whereas another 47 (25.5%) were probably so.

Emphasizing a point that will be made again in this book, Mark and Gath (1978) reported that in *every* case of children who were initially diagnosed psychiatric but were eventually shown to be neurologically impaired, declining school performance was an early indicator of the problem.

General Articles

Pless and Roghman (1971) found that 30% of chronically ill children (all illnesses) can be expected to show social or psychological maladjustment, which is significantly more than healthy children. A discussion of the neurological effects of cancer treatment with children was presented by Katz, Dolgin, and Varni (1990). Kopp and Kaler (1989) described physical risks to children from the mother's prepregnancy status to postnatal influences. For those of you interested in reading about the possible brain bases for disorders such as attention deficit disorders or dyslexia, two sources are recommended (Hynd & Semrud-Clikeman, 1989; Wicks-Nelson & Israel, 1991).

Conclusion

The main conclusion to be reached from this section is that we need more research about psychiatric symptoms in children and adolescents who are actually neurologically impaired. Beyond this, two points are noteworthy. First, any child or adolescent with a history of head injury or illness presents a special risk for psychiatric involvement. Second, based on the few studies available, children being brought for psychiatric help present a higher than usual rate of organic involvement and must be carefully screened.

BRAIN DYSFUNCTION AND THE NEUROSES

There are only a few articles in this section but they carry a consistent, powerful message to be careful about assuming psychiatric problems when dealing with patients who present with hysterical/conversion symptoms. As you will see, not uncommonly these vague physical complaints are early signs of brain impairment.

Comroe (1936) followed 100 patients who had been initially diagnosed as neurotic. He found that within 2 years or less (the average was 8 months), 24 patients showed clear signs of brain impairment. That is, at the time of the psychiatric diagnosis, 24% of the patients were actually showing early signs of brain dysfunction. The particular type of brain disorder varied considerably. Seven of the 100 patients died.

Consistent with Comroe's work, read what Plum and Posner (1982) wrote about hysteria. They noted, "Unfortunately, the diagnosis of psychogenic illness or hysteria often tells more about the physician's lack of knowledge than the patient's disease" (p. 305). Also, "For reasons not fully understood, 'hysterical' symptoms appear to be especially frequent in patients who turn out to have neurologic disorders" (p. 305). Finally, "psychogenic illness or hysteria [is] a diagnostic haven to which uncertain physicians all too often repair when signs and symptoms seem anatomically or physically senseless" (p. 305).

In 1965, Slater reported the results of 61 patients who were initially diagnosed as hysterical. Nearly half of these patients were eventually found to be suffering from an organic problem that fully explained their hysterical symptoms. Slater and Glithero (1965) followed 85 patients initially diagnosed as suffering from hysteria (of an original 99 patients, 14 could not be located). The follow-up was done in 1962 on patients from 1951, 1953, and 1955. Twelve patients had died, 4 by suicide and 8 from organic causes that Slater and Glithero concluded surely had to have been present at the time of the neurotic diagnosis. Nineteen patients were initially diagnosed as organic as well as hysterical. Twenty-two were initially diagnosed as purely hysterical but were later diagnosed as organic, whereas 32 of the 85 patients showed no signs of organic involvement at the time of follow-up.

In a report of a 10-year follow-up of 40 patients initially diagnosed as conversion disorders, Watson and Buranen (1979) found that 25% were ultimately found to be suffering some form of brain disorder. Whitlock (1967) compared 56 patients diagnosed as conversion disorder with 56 patients diagnosed as anxiety disorder or depression. At follow-up, 62.5% of the conversion patients had developed clear signs of brain involvement. Of the anxiety or depression group, 5.3% had developed such signs.

Conclusions

These few articles present a clear warning about being too quick to assume a psychiatric disorder when patients present with hysterical/conversion symptoms. The studies presented here show that with hysterical/conversion symptoms, one fourth or more of the patients may be expected to have some kind of neurological involvement. Although other forms of anxiety diagnoses are not excluded from scrutiny, those presenting with vague physical complaints such as weakness, or signs that mimic neurological disorders (e.g., areas of numbness or tingling, variable visual disturbances), must be carefully considered for neurological involvement even if the picture seems a classic psychiatric one.

ELDERLY PATIENTS

As I noted at the beginning of this chapter, many studies used a variety of ages of clients. In this section, the studies deal with the elderly patient. Elderly is not being specifically defined here: It refers to how the patients were described by the authors of the studies.

According to the Department of Health, Education and Welfare (1973), of people 65 years and older, 34.6% of those discharged from general hospitals carried a diagnosis of organic brain syndrome. Selzer and Sherwin (1978) noted that over 50% of geriatric psychiatric hospital admissions have organic diagnoses. Also, Selzer and Sherwin reported that 10% to 20% of the elderly living in the community have brain syndromes.

Carethers (1988) noted that between 3% and 10% of the elderly suffer from vitamin B-12 deficiency. This deficiency creates a number of neurological and psychiatric symptoms. Among the neurological symptoms, one is especially important: parathesias (areas of numbness). This is important because parathesias could easily be mistaken for conversion symptoms. Among the psychiatric symptoms of B-12 deficiency are dementia, delirium, psychosis, paranoia, irritability, depression, and personality change. Moss, D'Amico, and Maletta (1987) studied B-12 deficiency but also studied hypothyroidism and normal pressure hydrocephalus (essentially, enlarged ventricles with no increase in spinal fluid pressure), noting a wide range of psychiatric symptoms resulting from the physical disorders. Although dementia is a well-known brain impairment, Williamson et al. (1964) found that of 55 cases of dementia, in only 7 instances was the problem known to the patient's physician.

A subdural hematoma is a pool of blood, usually a clot, between the brain's outer lining, called the dura mater, and the lining just beneath it, called the arachnoid membrane. Stuteville and Welch (1958) studied 75 patients 65 years or older who had been diagnosed with a subdural hematoma. Beyond noting a propensity for the elderly to develop such a problem, usually from falls, the study noted that 12 patients (16%) were initially brought to the hospital because of mental or personality changes, not because of physical signs. As I noted in Chapter 1, and now is a good time to restate it, hematomas may be immediately evident or may not become apparent for days, weeks, or months after an injury.

Conclusions

It is obvious from this review that the elderly constitute a special at-risk population for neurological problems that present as psychiatric ones. Although most clinicians are familiar with certain forms of dementia (e.g., Alzheimer's), we must expand our knowledge of organic disorders among the elderly.

QUICK REVIEW AND COMMENTS ABOUT THE STUDIES IN THIS CHAPTER

Before summarizing these data, allow me to address some concerns that may have arisen in the course of reading this chapter. If you leave this chapter with a sense that the data are inconsistent or contradictory, it will be easier to downplay the importance of this material.

Variations Across Studies and What They Mean

As you read this chapter, the number of people in psychiatric treatment who actually suffered from an organic disorder varied considerably from study to study. There was considerable variation across studies in the number of patients for whom a medical condition was the direct cause of psychiatric symptoms. Do these wide variations nullify the results? Should we simply write off the studies as poor research and ignore them? The answer to both questions is "no." There are sound reasons for these variations.

First, the studies differed considerably in the mental health setting in which they were conducted. Some studies used psychiatric hospitals, some used emergency room patients, and some used outpatient settings.

It is not surprising that differences would occur across such divergent settings. For example, because state psychiatric hospitals tend to treat a large number of psychotic individuals, and certain brain disorders correlate highly with psychotic symptoms, it would be expected that these hospitals would have a higher rate than other settings.

Second, the studies addressed a wide variety of psychiatric diagnoses. Some studies focused on psychotic diagnoses, whereas others focused on hysterical disorders (both of which have a generally higher incidence of brain involvement). Other studies focused on a broad spectrum of diagnoses; therefore, we might expect a lower rate of neurological problems from those studies.

As a researcher I am impressed with the consistency of the literature. from 1894 to the present. Although specific data may vary from one study to another, the message remains the same: Clients in need of medical care are mistakenly being treated as if they have purely functional disorders.

SUMMARY

Two major conclusions may be reached from this review of the research. First, more than an occasional person who is seeking psychiatric help is in need of medical treatment. Referring to the rough calculations I presented in the General Survey section, it is not unreasonable to suggest that somewhere around 7% of the patients seeking psychiatric help have a medical illness that is directly causing the psychiatric symptoms, and that another 30% have a contributing physical illness. Before giving the estimates of 7% and 30% a definitiveness that is not warranted, it is crucial to remember that the rate of undiagnosed medical illnesses varied according to three major factors: age of the patient, type of psychiatric symptoms being presented, and location of psychiatric treatment (e.g., hospital). For some patients, medical treatment cured the psychiatric symptoms, whereas for others, medical treatment helped but did not eliminate the psychiatric concerns. It is equally clear from these studies that the large majority of people seeking psychiatric help do *not* have major physical problems, or, if they do, the medical problems are not contributing to the psychiatric picture. These data argue for a concerted effort at effective screening without an overreaction that leads to referring every client.

The second major conclusion to be drawn from the research is that, not surprisingly, the ability to detect a medical illness in a patient with psychiatric symptoms is related to the diagnostician's amount of medical training and everyday medical practice. In general, physicians do the best job of detecting medical problems, correctly diagnosing roughly two thirds of the cases. This is reasonable, given that physicians are trained in medical diagnosis. However, if the physician happens to be a psychiatrist, the success rate drops to about 50%. This is not especially surprising, given that many psychiatrists refer patients to other physicians for medical examination. McIntyre and Romano (1977) found that 32% of the psychiatrists they surveyed did not feel competent to perform a physical examination.

By the time the focus gets to nonmedical mental health workers, the success rate for recognizing a medical disorder drops to below 20%. Because nonmedical mental health professionals by definition are not trained in medicine, it is expected that their detection rates would be lower than their medical counterparts'. Whether or not the patient knows he or she has a medical problem depends on which study you read. Koran et al. (1989) found that 27% of the medical illnesses in their study were known to the client but not to the mental health system. Koranyi (1979) found that only 16% of the patients in his study were aware of their illness. In both studies, the rate of recognition by patients was not high.

SUGGESTED READINGS

For those of you who are interested in further reading about the interaction between organic and psychiatric conditions, in addition to a detailed reading of the articles that were presented in this chapter, I suggest the following books. Although some of the dates may seem a bit old, the books are well worth reading.

Begali, V. (1987). *Head injury in children and adolescents. A resource and review for school and allied professionals.* Brandon, VT: Clinical Psychology Publishing Company.

Benson, D. F., & Blumer, D. (Eds.). (1975). *Psychiatric aspects of neurological disease.* New York: Grune & Stratton.

Hynd, G. W., & Obrzut, J. E. (1981). *Neuropsychological assessment and the school age child.* New York: Grune & Stratton.

Jefferson, J. W., & Marshall, J. R. (1981). *Neuropsychiatric features of medical disorders.* New York: Plenum.

Lishman, W. (1978). *Organic psychiatry: The psychological consequences of cerebral disorder.* Oxford: Blackwell Scientific.

Roberts, J. K. A. (1984). *Differential diagnosis in neuropsychiatry.* Chichester: Wiley.

Strub, R. L., & Black, F. W. (1988). *Neurobehavioral disorders: A clinical approach.* Philadelphia: F. A. Davis.

Wells, C. E., & Duncan, G. W. (Eds.). (1980). *Neurology for psychiatrists.* Philadelphia: F. A. Davis.

3 THE SPECIAL ROLE OF THE MENTAL HEALTH PROFESSIONAL

This chapter addresses the special role of the mental health worker in screening for organic problems. It also addresses some of the questions that have probably arisen by now. The fact that mental health workers already possess a core of basic skills for screening will be emphasized in this chapter.

YOUR SPECIAL ROLE

The research presented in the previous chapter made it quite clear that the detection rate of medical illnesses in psychiatric clients needs to be improved. The role of the mental health professional in these cases is clear. The mental health worker is on the front line. Clients, having no reason to suspect a medical problem, are turning to the mental health system because of their psychiatric complaints. The problem of misdiagnosis is not new; it was noted at the end of the last century. The difference between then and now is that increased knowledge of brain function has allowed a greater awareness of potential organic problems among psychiatric clients. Acknowledging this potential for organic problems, before clients are accepted into mental health care, it is our responsibility to determine that the problem is, in fact, a psychiatric one. This is not something about which the mental health field has an option. We have no choice but to become skilled in screening for organic disorders. Hypothetically, there is a way around this but it is hardly a feasible alternative.

We could absolutely require that all patients have a complete medical examination, including a neurological examination, before entering psychiatric treatment. Many authors cited in the previous chapter suggested a medical examination as a routine part of the diagnostic process. Although I certainly endorse the idea of a medical examination prior to treatment, I might add that ideally it would be desirable to have neuropsychological results, as well. Of course, most of the clients would either be healthy or would have physical problems unrelated to their psychiatric ones. However, I would rather have a healthy person undergo an "unnecessary" medical examination than have a person in psychological treatment who, in fact, is physically ill.

Although there is an ideal, preferable process, I am pragmatic and realistic. I know that a required medical examination is not a realistic option in many situations. In some cases, for example, psychiatric emergencies, an examination is not usually possible, yet this may be the only time you see the person. In other cases, the person either will not cooperate or cannot afford such an examination (more on this in Chapter 8). It is apparent we cannot force a client to undergo a medical examination if he or she refuses. It is equally apparent that we cannot require a client who has little or no money to see a physician for a thorough medical examination. This is not to say that we should ignore physical signs in a client (of course, we must do our best to refer the person if the situation clearly warrants it); it is to say that we should have some good reason for suggesting the referral. In other words, mental health professionals must become proficient in screening for organic disorders. This is a task for which we are ideally suited.

ACCEPTING A CERTAIN RISK

Throughout this book the emphasis is on the term *screening*. It is important to keep in mind that the mental health professional's job is not to diagnose and treat physical illnesses. This is the task of the physician. It is the role of the mental health worker to help decide who should and should not be referred for a more thorough assessment.

By definition, screening is a process in which one accepts a certain risk of not detecting all of the target cases. One must trade off the risk of missing cases against the realities of staff time, budgets, probabilities of problems, and the needs of patients. If the admission process for mental health care included a complete medical examination, complete neurological examination, complete social history, several interviews, several observation periods, and comprehensive psychological testing of every client, we would not need a screening program. The risk of missing a physically ill client would be reduced to almost nothing if such a program were required, but, even then there would still be *some* risk. Obviously, without immense investments in staff and time, such a procedure is not even close to realistic. This leaves the alternative of a screening procedure.

Having decided that screening is the only realistic possibility, the next decision is to establish an acceptable success rate for the procedure. I do not mean this in a formal, statistical fashion. That is, we do not have to come up with a precise figure (even if that were possible). It does mean that the more involved the screening procedure, the greater will be its success rate—if the procedures themselves are carefully selected.

With or without any additional formal screening procedures, there is a great deal you can do as an individual mental health professional. You can become acquainted with the major signs of brain disorders and you can learn who is a likely candidate for further evaluation. Of course, the unfortunate fact is that no individual or program will detect every case of undiagnosed physical problems. The mental health field does not have the luxury of the kind of precision that is needed to attain a perfect detection rate. Nonetheless, we can certainly improve on the success rates we now have.

IS SCREENING A DIFFICULT TASK TO LEARN?

As I noted in Chapter 1, the question is invariably going to arise as to whether this is the type of skill that can be easily acquired by mental health professionals. The answer is an unequivocal "yes." To do this type of screening requires keeping in mind the nature of your role. Your role is to recognize that a client *may* have a problem requiring further investigation. You do not have to be familiar with medical terminology or to understand Latin to be able to *screen* effectively for organic disorders. You will be screening, not diagnosing. Detailed knowledge is not required to know that something is wrong. Consider the following two examples.

It is a safe assumption that most of you own an automobile. You have basic knowledge of how the automobile works and how it should and should not sound. If you are driving down the road and all of a sudden a new and ominous noise occurs, you assume something is wrong with the car. When you get in your car and it will not start, you know something is wrong with it. Do you have to be a skilled automobile mechanic to understand that something is wrong? Of course not. All you need is the ability to recognize *that* something is wrong—not necessarily *what* is wrong.

Where would we be if we had to call the garage and specify the exact problem before the mechanic would work on it? Would that not nullify the need for most mechanics? After all, if we already know enough to diagnose the problem correctly, there is a good chance we could fix it (time permitting, etc.). The point is that we do not have to have any detailed knowledge of the internal combustion engine or other automobile systems to be able to recognize that something is wrong. Of course, the more we know, the greater the chance that we will detect a problem in its earliest stages. However, we have to decide just how much time and energy we want to spend learning about automobiles to enable us to detect a problem early in its course. For most of us, a passing acquaintance with automobiles is enough. We will do the screening and then turn the automobile over to the expert mechanic and let her or him decide precisely what is wrong.

Another example, closer to the purpose of this book, is that you do not have to have a degree in medicine to recognize, in most cases, that someone is sick. The simple presence of a fever or a painful area indicates a problem. We know that the person may need to see a physician. We do not need an M.D. or D.O. to be able to tell that much. Of course, the more we know about medicine, the more likely we are to recognize signs of an illness, even those not readily or obviously apparent. Further, the more we know about medicine the more likely we are to diagnose the problem correctly. Most of us do not have medical degrees, but for the sake of our own health we must have enough knowledge at least to screen for medical illness. We must be able to judge which symptoms can be left to run their course, which ones can be treated at home, and which ones require medical attention. At a slightly more sophisticated level, this is all that is expected of the mental health professional in the screening process.

It is evident that the more you know the more likely you are to screen for physical problems effectively. You will have to decide how much time and energy can be devoted to studying the topic. You will have to decide how much is enough knowledge to do a competent job in your setting. Fortunately, acquiring sufficient knowledge of screening procedures is not as time consuming as you might first imagine. Your training to become a mental health professional has already provided you with a number of important skills that are required to screen effectively.

BASIC SKILLS

Given that you already possess many of the skills that are required to screen for brain problems, all that remains is to acquire basic knowledge of the diagnostic signs that will raise the question of organicity. It is now simply a matter of combining existing skills with new knowledge. What you will be doing is not significantly different from what you do now. You will slightly shift the emphasis of signs for which you look. The skills you already possess are your knowledge of psychiatric disorders, your interviewing skills, and your observation skills.

Knowledge of Psychiatric Disorders

This is a given. To be in the mental health field one must understand psychiatric problems. By this, I do not mean strictly in the diagnostic sense. I am referring to a general knowledge of the disorders. Not only do you know the typical symptoms, but you are familiar with possible causal events, and you are familiar with the usual course of the illness (under what conditions it starts and how long it lasts). You are already familiar with typical responses to treatment. All of this knowledge is important to the screening process because variations from the expected patterns can be a sign that further investigation is required. Simply stated, if there is not a good fit between what *ought to be* and what *is,* a sign of possible organicity has been detected. It is understood that no two clients are exactly alike, but it is also understood that for clients to share a common psychiatric diagnosis they must share certain qualities that define the disorder. It is the shared factors that require our special attention.

Interviewing

You already know how to interview, and this is one of the most important aspects of the screening process. You are already a trained listener, and you are alert for discrepancies and inconsistencies in the client's report. Asking the right questions and knowing when to probe and when enough is already known are hallmarks of an effective interviewer. In the case of screening for brain disorders, you will use these skills as you ask certain types of questions and as you carefully listen to the client. The questions to be asked and the material of interest for this purpose are presented in Chapters 4 through 7.

Observation

You are already a trained observer of people. This ability is critical in screening. As the material in Chapter 5 will make clear, an immense amount of information can be obtained by simply watching the person in the interview and other settings. None of the physical factors presented in this book requires specialized training or equipment for detection. They only require that you be aware of them. You will focus on observing certain types of behaviors and physical signs as you screen for organicity.

In two words, what you already bring to the screening process are *clinical skills*. The skills remain the same in screening for organicity. All that is added is a new set of signs aimed specifically toward detection of clients with brain disorders.

SCREENING THE LONG-TERM CLIENT

What about the case of the long-term client? Is screening still necessary, given that the person has probably been examined many times? Is it finally safe to assume the problem is purely psychological? No, it is not safe to assume a purely psychological problem, and screening is still most certainly in order. Screening for brain problems is just as critical in this case as in any other case. There are three main reasons for this.

First, it is unwise to assume automatically that previous diagnoses were correct. After all, this book is based on the premise that too many people are misdiagnosed as psychiatric. Long-running diagnoses tend to have been built on each other, with the latest diagnosis reflecting the influence of earlier ones. As several studies in Chapter 2 showed, some patients had carried psychiatric diagnoses for years before a correct medical diagnosis was made. Always treat a long-term patient as a new one. Knowing the history of the person is always important, but let the present diagnosis stand on its own merit.

Second, the fact that the psychiatric symptoms have gone on for so long should make you wonder about the possibility of organic involvement. Most psychological problems respond to treatment, medical or psychological. Should we not be a bit suspicious of a problem that does not respond to treatment? Of course, a lack of therapeutic response does not guarantee the existence of an organic disease. A number of other possibilities can be raised for why a person does not get better. These other factors must be considered, but not to the exclusion of organic possibilities.

Third, the very fact that the client is long-term means he or she is getting older (realizing that some young people can be long-term clients). Being long-term means he or she has a greater possibility of having been exposed to conditions that could create brain disorders, such as excess consumption of alcohol, falls, or exposure to toxins. With increasing age come increased probabilities of brain diseases (e.g., certain kinds of tumors or strokes). Also with increasing age come increased probabilities of other medical illnesses that may contribute to brain dysfunction (e.g., diabetes and cancer). In other words, even if the psychiatric diagnosis was initially correct, the possibility of organic involvement cannot be ruled out in the present. There is no rule that says a psychiatric patient cannot develop a brain tumor or incur a stroke or be injured in a fall.

TWO POINTS TO REMEMBER

Before closing this chapter, two points about effective screening must be discussed. One point is that you need to set realistic expectations about what can and cannot be accomplished with screening. The second point is that you have to shift your mental set slightly from purely psychological to the possibility of organic factors.

Realistic Expectations

As I have noted several times, no screening efforts will be able to detect all cases of organic involvement. For that matter, even sophisticated programs are going to miss cases every now and then. You cannot expect the impossible. One guaranteed way to fail is to set expectations so high that no one can reach them. To expect a 100% accuracy rate in screening would be just such an expectation. Our present state of knowledge about psychiatric disorders and brain function is too limited to allow 100% accuracy. Therefore, the inability to detect all cases simply has to be tolerated as a sign of the field's lack of knowledge. We can only do as well as prevailing knowledge and conditions allow. The clear premise of this and other books, though, is that we can do a great deal better than we have in the past.

Mental Set

It is no secret that what people expect to find has an influence on what they do find. Research from a number of areas clearly shows this (e.g., the placebo effect). We in the mental health field are not immune to this tendency. Having been told in advance that a client has certain characteristics, it is not surprising that those characteristics are again seen: We have been primed to look for them. The actions and words of the client will be interpreted in light of what is expected. For example, having been informed that a client was previously diagnosed as schizophrenic, any peculiarity of speech will be interpreted as a sign of thought disorganization. If we had been told the client was diagnosed with post-traumatic stress disorder, that same peculiarity of speech would be seen in a different light.

It is probable that if we are looking for psychological factors we are more likely to see them because we directly or subtly exclude other possibilities. Because most practitioners in the mental health field lean toward psychological explanations, they must make a special effort to be aware of this and to entertain other possibilities (rather than immediately assume a psychological problem). The tendency to feel confident about a psychological disorder is especially prevalent when a client presents a classic, textbook symptom picture. Under these conditions, the tendency is immediately to rule out other possibilities: The fit between expected and observed is so close that other explanations seem unnecessary. I must, however, caution against this tendency. Many of the studies presented in Chapter 2 described patients with classic psychological symptoms who were later discovered to have brain impairment (especially the hysteria/conversion and schizophrenia diagnoses).

The fact that a client presents classic signs of a psychiatric disorder does not automatically mean that it is psychogenic. Therefore, we must force ourselves to entertain other possibilities. Even if we are relatively sure of a psychogenic problem, what is lost other than a little time in considering physical explanations? Given the ramifications of a missed diagnosis, it is difficult to justify not taking the time to consider organicity.

Simply stated, remain open to all possibilities. Our present state of knowledge does not allow the luxury of endorsing one approach over another. Look beyond preferred options and consider other possible explanations for the client's problems.

THE FIRST THREE CHAPTERS: SETTING THE STAGE

The first three chapters have set the stage for the remainder of the book. There is an unmistakable message that we in the mental health field have no choice but to improve our ability to screen for brain problems (and all other medical conditions, I might add). The research shows a remarkably consistent picture of organic problems that present as psychiatric disorders, sometimes with amazing similarity to classic psychiatric symptom pictures. These occurrences are, as you know by now, far from rare. The consequences of missing an organic case and treating it as a psychiatric one are serious.

It is obvious that mental health professionals have a special role in the screening process. Clients with what they believe to be psychiatric conditions (or, in some cases, what friends, relatives, or other professionals believe to be psychiatric) will naturally turn to the mental health field for help. Fortunately, mental health workers already have certain basic skills needed for screening. All that remains is to become aware of the signs that should raise the question of organic involvement.

4 SCREENING: A CAREFUL HISTORY OF THE CLIENT

Whenever I speak to a professional group or talk to one of my classes on the topic of undiagnosed brain disorders in psychiatric clients, the question invariably arises as to what the mental health professional can do to detect such problems (assuming the worker has no special or detailed knowledge of the brain). I answer this by noting that a great deal can be done, but that two points stand out above all others. First, know as much as possible about the general signs of brain impairment. Obviously, the more one knows about the brain, the better the chance of detecting a problem. Second, take a careful, detailed history of the client. There is no doubt that a thorough history of the client is one of the best screening techniques available.

As would be expected in any other mental health history, an accurate history is best obtained by talking not only to the client but to other people who know him or her. The client's perception of the situation may or not correspond to how other people see it. Discrepancies in accounts are indicators that further inquiry is needed. It is also most helpful to obtain any corroborating information that is available, such as previous psychological evaluations, medical records, or other information that will be of help in getting an accurate impression of the client. Although the client and his or her family may remember the general details of past difficulties, the *specific* details may be of great significance. Obtaining actual reports will allow access to information or impressions that may not have been shared with the client or family.

Beyond the rather obvious reasons for involving other people and corroborating information in a client's social and medical history, there is a specific reason when the possibility of brain impairment is being investigated. The reason is that one of the most common effects of brain disorder is memory impairment. One can hardly expect to get an accurate history from a person whose memory is suspect. It is not advisable to assume that the client's memory loss will be readily apparent to the interviewer. The loss may range from hardly noticeable to blatantly obvious.

Having worked in a number of mental health settings myself, I am quite aware that sometimes no one is available to provide another perspective on the problem. Also, in some cases, the client will not give permission to contact other people. There is no way around this problem. The client has a right to confidentiality. Under these circumstances, you need to be especially vigilant for inconsistencies or discrepancies within the client's own account and between his or her account and any available information. Do not assume that inconsistencies or discrepancies between the client's account and other information are necessarily the result of purposeful deception or cognitive impairment. Over the years I have, as I am sure you have, come across numerous examples of conflicting details in previous records. Records from different agencies or practitioners may present widely discrepant information on the details of the client's history. A single report may even contain such errors (for example, placing the client in two different places during the same time span). Always ask the client about discrepancies.

In obtaining information on the topics to be presented in this chapter, you need only follow your usual interviewing procedures. There is no special sequence this interview must follow; how it is conducted is really up to you and the style with which you feel most comfortable. All you are really going to do is add a few questions to your usual ones and be looking for certain important indicators.

MEDICAL HISTORY

It is of the utmost importance that you inquire about medical illnesses, both those that involve the brain directly and those that affect the brain but are primarily diseases of other parts of the body. In conducting this inquiry, be sensitive to the level of the client's understanding about such problems. Use everyday terminology and translate whenever necessary, rather than assuming the client knows the formal name of a disease. Be careful about how you ask the questions and the words you use. Asking a client if he or she has ever had a serious illness depends on whose definition of serious you are using. I learned fairly early in my career never to ask questions in this way when a client I had interviewed for about an hour happened to note, almost parenthetically, just prior to his leaving that he was on rather large dosages of insulin (I had asked about serious health problems, of course). His view of the illness was that it was not serious; therefore, he saw no reason to mention it. He got along very well, he said. A reply that one has never had a head injury does not necessarily mean the client has not had one; it only means that he or she may not be aware of having had one. Throughout the topics presented here, I will point out when special inquiry might be needed.

As you go through the medical topics in the following list, remember you are not required to have extensive knowledge about them. The purpose here is to know when to refer a person for a medical evaluation; to do that does not require detailed knowledge of medical diagnoses. Your task is to ask the right questions and to follow up the responses to your satisfaction. The client does not know what it is you need to know, so the onus is on you to be sure you get the necessary information. By the time your interview and review of material is complete, you should be able to address each of the medical points in this section. Just how you choose to obtain the information is a matter for you to decide. During my neuropsychology internship I was provided a checklist of important medical disorders which I read to each client, making detailed inquiry when necessary. I still use this list. You may decide that the client's last medical examination or his or her reported history of good health rules out the necessity of such a checklist. However you obtain the information, know whether or not your client has had (or has) any of the conditions described below. The following topics are not in order of importance. They are equally important.

Regularity of Medical Care

Inquire if the person has a family physician and if medical examinations take place on a schedule appropriate for the person's physical condition and age. Ask when the last complete physical examination was completed and what procedures were included in it. Was it a routine office physical, or were additional tests ordered (e.g., a CT scan)? The utilization of special procedures may indicate that the physician suspected something. Ascertain the results of the examination. If there are frequent visits to the physician, be sure to find out why. If it has been a long time since the last visit, you also want to know why. Perhaps the client is having symptoms and is afraid to go to the physician for fear of what may be discovered.

Hospitalization

Always ask if the person has been hospitalized at any time in his or her life. Of course, you need the details. Why was the client hospitalized? What was the outcome? Were there changes in the person's psychological state before, during, or after the hospital stay? What kinds of treatments were provided? Even if the person reports the hospital stay as "nothing," be sure to ask what symptoms led to the hospital stay. If the hospital care was required because of an accident (automobile or otherwise), be sure to get the details. Even if no head injury was specifically reported, the client may describe conditions that make it a high likelihood, such as describing a dazed condition after a fall.

Surgery

Has the person ever had surgery, and why? Even if it did not involve the brain directly, the reason for surgery may give you a clue about conditions that may affect the brain (e.g., cancer). In addition, there is always the possibility of oxygen deprivation, reactions to anesthetic agents, and blood clotting (which can lead to blockage of blood supply to the brain). As was noted in the previous section, if the surgery was required because of an injury, have the person describe the situation as well as he or she can. Just because the brain was not directly involved does not mean it escaped injury.

Brain Impairment

Ask the client if he or she has ever had any kind of diagnosed brain problem, but also ask if he or she has ever been unconscious for any reason, received a blow to the head, or has ever suspected a brain problem for any reason. A client's suspicion of brain problems does not constitute a diagnosis but it can lead to a description of symptoms that might cause you to wonder. If some of these questions seem unnecessary, consider a study by Carlsson (1986) in which it was found that about 20% of people who had been rendered unconscious *did not* seek medical help. Research is available that shows even minor injuries can have notable effects for months afterward (e.g., Rimel, Giordini, Barth, Boll, & Jane, 1981). It is important to know that the cumulative effects of several minor injuries can easily add up to serious brain damage. However, one injury is enough to cause problems, so do not be lulled into a false sense of security because it was "a long time ago" and "it only happened once."

Be sure to ask if the client has a history of seizures. Find out if medical care was obtained, and if diagnosis and treatment occurred. Any history of seizures must be explored with the client to determine if further examination is warranted (e.g., infant seizures during a high fever, called febrile seizures, usually have no serious sequelae). It is important to ask the client about any accidents (automobile or otherwise) that might have involved injury to the brain. Even if the accident did not apparently involve the brain directly, ask for details. The brain is so fragile that injury can occur easily; therefore, any accident should be suspect. It is quite possible to incur an injury and not know it, or to have been told that everything was fine when, in fact, it was not. Take, for example, a person who incurs brain damage on the job and returns to the same job (which happens to be repetitive and mostly manual). This person may genuinely report no obvious effects after the injury. However, a few years later when he or she decides to go to college or to a vocational school, the effects of the damage become apparent for the first time. The person's verbal memory problem *now* becomes evident. The problem was there all along, but the situation did not make it apparent. Any history of brain injury or illness must be carefully considered in light of the client now seeking mental health services.

Any history of fainting (syncope, dizziness) should be explored. Fainting not only raises questions about why it happened; there is always the possibility of a head injury when the person falls. Do not assume that because a person has had these experiences, he or she will have sought medical attention. Fainting, near-fainting, or dizziness can result from a number of innocuous conditions, but it is not for us to assume what might have caused the symptoms.

Cancer

A history of cancer is important for two reasons. First, some of the treatments (e.g., chemotherapy) involve powerful drugs or are otherwise capable of potentially producing problems (e.g., surgery). Most important, however, is that the cancer can metastacize (spread to other parts of the body), typically via the bloodstream. Approximately 6% of brain tumors are metastatic (Adams & Victor, 1985). Adams and Victor reported that certain forms of cancer are more likely than others to metastacize to the brain. In order of frequency, they are lung, breast, melanoma, the GI tract, and kidney. Adams and Victor further noted that other forms of cancer may metastacise, but that cancer of the prostate, esophagus, oropharynx, and skin (other than melanoma) rarely do so. Without trying to remember all of this, it is as simple as questioning the possibility of organicity if there is a history of cancer—any cancer. Do not, then, be too quick to assume that a cancer patient's psychological concerns are necessarily a result of the stress of having such a serious condition.

Lung Problems

The general term for these diseases is COPD (Chronic Obstructive Pulmonary Disease). Lung problems of any nature that are serious enough to interfere appreciably with breathing are important because the brain uses roughly 20% of the oxygen in the body. Any condition that restricts the flow of air to the lungs, or adversely influences oxygen absorption, is affecting how much oxygen gets to the brain. The brain dies within minutes if oxygen is completely cut off; however, in the case of COPD, oxygen is not completely cut off but is chronically in short supply to the brain. Chronic lung diseases such as emphysema, asthma, and bronchitis warrant special inquiry.

Although not technically a lung problem per se, ask about any situation in which breathing would have been stopped or impaired for a significant time. Examples of such situations would be a near drowning, near strangulation for any reason, high altitude oxygen deprivation, or resuscitation after a medical crisis (such as being revived on the operating table). Unless it was an unusual case, the typical childhood experience of having "the wind knocked out of you" would be no cause for concern.

You will have to use your judgment as to whether or not a given experience warrants further concern and investigation. In general, there is no great reason for concern if the time of oxygen deprivation was less than a minute or two, but after that, concern is warranted.

Heart Conditions

Heart conditions are important because a malfunction of the heart affects blood circulation, which means lowered levels of oxygen and glucose to the brain. There is also the possibility of blood clots forming and then breaking loose to travel through the blood stream to the brain. The clot blocks off blood supply to the affected area of the brain (a stroke). A history of heart attacks is noteworthy because such an attack involves impaired blood flow to the brain. Of course, if there have been multiple heart attacks, the chances of damage to the brain increase each time. Include, in your questioning, childhood diseases that affect the heart, for example, scarlet fever or rheumatic fever.

Hypertension

Hypertension (high blood pressure) can result in a number of dangerous health conditions, but here the concern is with stroke. The continued pressure against blood vessel walls can weaken them to the point that they balloon up in an especially weak area (called an aneurysm). If this weak area bursts, a stroke has occurred. Although hypertension is noted for producing essentially no noticeable symptoms, some people will experience hypertension headaches. These are typically located at the back of the head, and correspond to increases in blood pressure. A history of hypertension is common among patients diagnosed as having multi-infarct dementia.

Blood Diseases

The concern here is with diseases that are likely to affect the blood-stream's ability to carry oxygen or glucose to the brain; for example, anemia resulting in hypoxia (low oxygen). Also, there is concern with those diseases that are likely to result in a clotting condition, and those that result in blocking of blood vessels (e.g., high cholesterol levels or any other arteriosclerotic condition), thus cutting off needed supplies for brain functioning.

Diabetes

Diabetes actually refers to a number of conditions involving abnormal levels of blood sugar (glucose). There are two major concerns with a diabetic condition. First, blood vessels themselves can be directly affected, thus interfering with the brain's blood supply (a point that has been addressed several times already). Second, because the brain gets its energy from glucose, variations in glucose level will affect function. Parenthetically, I might note that the brain's use of glucose is just like any other system of the body. The harder it works, the more glucose it uses. This is part of the basis for the fatigue we feel when we have exerted ourselves mentally (studying, doing psychotherapy, or mulling over a tragic event). The energy we use for mental activity is the same as the energy we use for physical activity.

High levels of glucose (hyperglycemia) and low glucose levels (hypoglycemia) can produce myriad psychological symptoms. These range from irritability to depression to confusion to intoxication-like states.

Endocrine Disturbances

Any problem in the endocrine system is capable of wreaking psychological havoc. Certainly, some of the best known problems in this category involve the thyroid gland (several studies in Chapter 2 dealt with this). Symptoms of hyper- or hypothyroid conditions range from depressive to neurotic to manic-like. Disturbances of the sex-related hormones are well known, and have been implicated in a number of conditions (e.g., aggressiveness, irritability, and poorly controlled emotions).

Electrolyte Imbalance

Electrolytes are substances in the body that are related to the transmission of electrical impulses. Common ones are sodium and potassium. Deficiencies in these elements can result in such symptoms as dizziness, confusion, or muscle weakness. In essence, the nerve impulses cannot be conducted as they should. This problem is especially noteworthy with people who are taking certain kinds of medications that deplete these elements (e.g., certain medications for hypertension deplete potassium).

Eating Habits

Is the person on an unsupervised, unusual diet for any reason? Unsupervised diets can be dangerous because certain substances needed for normal operation of the body may be deficient (e.g., the electrolytes discussed in the previous section), or there may be excesses of some element. The reason for the special diet is not important: The body does not care *why* important elements are deficient. This factor may certainly include anorexia and bulimia, but your inquiry must not be limited to them. Perhaps the person is on some kind of self-prescribed "health" diet that excludes a needed nutrient or results in an excess of some substance. Perhaps the person is on a "crash" diet, or is fasting excessively. Ask about changes in appetite and weight. Has appetite diminished drastically, or, inversely, has it become voracious? Changes in appetite may reflect any number of physical or psychological states, including brain disorders. Perhaps the person consumes unusually large amounts of water or other fluids. Excess consumption of water (water intoxication) not only affects brain function—it can be fatal (e.g., Illowsky & Kirch, 1988; Vieweg et al., 1985).

Electrical Shock

Because a strong electrical shock can stop the heart and lungs from functioning, brain damage can occur if the stoppage lasts more than a few minutes. There is, of course, the possibility of direct brain damage from the shock or from a related fall. It follows that if the shock did not result in a fall or heart or lung stoppage, the chances of brain damage are diminished, but take nothing for granted.

High Fevers

The brain cannot tolerate more than a few degrees elevation in temperature for any prolonged time before damage occurs. Ask how high the fever was, what caused it, and, especially, how long it lasted. If the fever remained below 104 or 105 for a relatively brief time, the need for concern diminishes. Sustained or unexplained high fevers must always be further explored with the client, even if a considerable amount of time has elapsed since the fever.

While on the topic of high temperatures, note that sunstroke/heatstroke is a dangerous condition that can result in brain damage. Ask the person if he or she was examined for brain functions and if any residual effects from the episode are known. I referred a person because of an episode of heatstroke. The neurologist concluded there were no sequelae. Was the referral a waste of time? Of course not. The question had to be answered.

Birth

It is most important to ask about birth. Was it complicated in any way? What was the infant's health at the time of birth? If the birth was considerably premature, the infant presents a special risk. Did the mother consume alcohol or other drugs during pregnancy? Did the mother have any serious medical illnesses during pregnancy? Of course, there are two major concerns here. First, the possibility of direct brain damage from the birth process itself or from a cutoff of oxygen and blood to the baby. Second, there is the possibility of poor brain development as a result of the mother suffering an illness or injury, suffering a poor diet, or using drugs (prescribed or not) that might affect fetal brain development.

Sexually Transmitted Diseases

In terms of brain impairment, the major STD of concern is syphilis. If this seems of historical value only, syphilis is on the increase (e.g., Adams & Victor, 1985). I tested a man with neurosyphilis during my postdoctoral internship 6 years ago. Between 5% and 10% of untreated syphilis cases will develop neurosyphilis (also known as general paresis). Although AIDS is transmitted by means other than sexual, it is important to realize that the disease often produces dementia.

Infections

Infections may spread to the brain from other sites or may begin within the brain or its surrounding tissues, creating problems such as meningitis (infection of the meninges—the outer coverings of the brain) or encephalitis (infection within the brain). Sometimes the brain as a whole is involved; sometimes only localized areas of infection occur. Onset of psychological symptoms following a serious infection needs to be investigated. In most cases of meningitis or encephalitis the medical symptoms are so obvious that medical attention is ensured; however, one should not assume that all such cases were detected and treated. Never assume that aftereffects related to infection-produced brain damage have been diagnosed.

Numbness or Weakness

Ask if the person has (or has had) areas of numbness, either transient or ongoing. Related to this, ask if the person has any areas of tingling sensations (or similar descriptions). Be sure to ask about unexplained weakness such as difficulty holding a pencil, or difficulty maintaining movements that were once easily executed. Even if the person does show characteristics of hysteria, do not assume these symptoms are conversion disorders or the fears of a hypochondriac.

Toxins

This is a difficult topic for most clients to address because they are likely to be unaware of exposure in many cases (and we are still learning just how dangerous some chemicals are). Nonetheless, ask if the person was ever exposed to toxins of any kind. For example, being overcome by natural gas or by automobile exhaust (carbon monoxide), or exposure to such substances as lead, mercury, insecticides, solvents, cleaning agents, or lawn and farm chemicals. Strub and Black (1988) present an excellent chapter on the topic of toxins. Anderson (1982) and Roberts (1984) also offer extended discussions about toxic substances that are likely to produce neurological symptoms.

MEDICATIONS

Any medication, prescribed or over the counter (OTC), has the potential to produce a wide spectrum of psychiatric symptoms. Ironically, psychiatric medications may produce their own psychiatric symptoms while they alleviate others. Questioning about medications must take into account several factors. It does not matter that a drug is an OTC medication. It is just as capable of producing depression, confusion, or anxiety as a prescription medication. Also, there are immense differences in how people are affected by drugs. Because of physiological differences, what to one person may be an ineffective dose could be an overdose to another person; therefore, do not let recommended dosages mislead you.

The older a person is, the more likely he or she is to be overmedicated by the same dosage that at one time was quite adequate. Because of changes in how the body utilizes medications, most elderly people should have a careful check to see if their dosage needs to be reduced. Regardless of age, there is the problem of drug interactions. Two or more drugs combined can produce symptoms that neither one alone would have produced. In essence, the mixture is producing a new drug. This includes any mixture of prescription drugs, OTC drugs, and alcohol or other drugs. Include in your inquiry asking about any "health" medications such as megadoses of vitamins and minerals and other substances. Excesses of some of these can be fatal (e.g., vitamin D), while others may produce psychotic symptoms (e.g., vitamin A).

It is imperative that you ascertain the medications the person takes regularly or occasionally, and what symptoms precipitated the use of the drug. Also, determine if the onset of psychological symptoms correlates with the medication. Be careful in your inquiry that you do not suggest a relationship between symptoms and the medication. Let the client's discussion, guided by your questions, answer it for you. There is no way in the brief confines of a book such as this that one could describe all the possible psychiatric symptoms that may result from medications. You need to have a drug compendium as a reference and take the time to look up your clients' drugs and the drugs' common effects. Sources are available on OTC drugs and on drug interactions. Do not assume the client knows about these effects and interactions. He or she may not have been told or may not have paid close enough attention when the topic was discussed.

ONSET OF THE PROBLEM

There is certainly nothing new about asking about this, but the emphasis should be on several points. A critical emphasis here is on whether or not the psychiatric symptoms developed according to the usual psychological course. Simply stated, does the description of the onset fit the pattern it should fit? If not, you should be suspicious. For example, the onset of psychotic symptoms for the first time in a person over 40 or so should make you wonder. Onset of "hysterical" symptoms after a medical diagnosis of a serious illness should be carefully investigated. Recent attention problems in a young person who had a "minor" football concussion 1 month ago are probably more than coincidence. Onset of anxiety after a person started taking a certain medication is too obvious to be overlooked. An unexplained change in social or personality habits of a person who underwent surgery a year ago is a bit too much to be ignored.

Essentially, you have to know the typical course of psychological problems and their likely history. Then you see how closely your client fits this. Is the person too young or too old to fit the usual case? Is the course of the problem a bit too far from the usual course? Does the problem usually have a precipitator, yet your client has none?

Our present knowledge about mental disorders is far from complete, especially in terms of causes. Wide variations from person to person are expected. You must use your clinical judgment to decide if the variations you see are too great to be considered within the expected range. Peculiarities of onset are not guarantees of organicity, but they do raise it as a possibility.

SUBSTANCE ABUSE

A history of substance abuse presents special concern for the possibility of brain impairment. There is the ever-present potential for direct brain damage from the substance itself or from related problems such as poor diet. The destructive effects of many drugs on the brain are well known. An equally important reason for a careful inquiry about substance abuse is that people who are using alcohol and other drugs may incur brain damage as a result of falling, being hit on the head during a fight, or from an accident. The typical closed head injury victim is a young man who has been drinking and has an automobile accident. Of course, the longer one has been involved in substance abuse, the greater the likelihood of brain impairment, but once is enough in some cases.

Establishing whether or not a person has abused drugs is not easy (I worked for a year on an alcoholism unit). Because denial is such a common characteristic of the problem, coupled with the fact that the subtances may be illegal, descriptions of use are frequently several degrees from the truth. It is especially important here to talk to someone else, such as a spouse or children, to try to ascertain the degree of use. Pay special attention to prescription drugs that are being abused. Skillful questioning is a necessity here. Reading between the lines also becomes a useful skill. How many times have you heard some variation of "I drink a little now and then"?

OCCUPATION

This is a factor that is too easily dismissed. It must be explored carefully. Certain occupations present a high risk of neurological involvement. Farming, for example, is a very dangerous occupation, not only because of the machinery, but also because of the frequent exposure to toxic chemicals in the form of insecticides and herbicides. Two types of occupations warrant especially close investigation: those involving toxins and those involving a high likelihood of falls or other forms of blows to the head (e.g., some types of construction). Include in your list of occupations involving toxins those that are likely to affect lung performance (e.g., mining). Anderson (1982) estimated that 20 million Americans work with neurotoxic substances. (See the earlier section in this chapter on toxins.) Learn to ask about chemicals in the workplace. Do not assume they are not present.

Ask the client to describe his or her job and the types of materials with which he or she comes into contact. Be sure to ask about previous jobs. Just because the present one does not suggest a great risk does not mean that past ones were safe. If the person was in the military, ask about job specifics and about combat experiences.

Even if the job has established safety standards for protective gear or similar measures, do not assume they were followed. As one example of toxic exposure, Strub and Black (1988) mentioned the possibility of a painter not using appropriate protection from fumes. I saw just such an instance several years ago. I went to pick up an automobile that had been painted by a professional. The person acted as if he was drunk. It became apparent that he had painted the car without using a mask or proper ventilation. He was intoxicated from paint and solvent fumes.

Being a good interviewer about occupation basically requires a commonsense approach to the possibility of the job creating neurological problems. Two good sources for detailed information about this topic are Anderson (1982) for neurotoxins and Roberts (1984) for both neurotoxins and at-risk occupations.

LIFE-STYLE

Questions about the client's life-style are aimed at uncovering potentially hazardous actions other than those occurring at work. For example, inquiry about hobbies may reveal that the person is an amateur boxer. I tested a man who had been an amateur boxer for a few years. By the time I saw him many years later he showed the classic physical and cognitive signs of dementia pugilistica (the punch-drunk syndrome). Although this disorder is at the extreme, anyone who receives blows to the head is at risk. Even though once is enough to kill, in most cases, the damage is cumulative over many blows. The person who fights also may be someone who gets in bar fights, for instance, having nothing to do with formal hobbies.

Does the person ride motorcycles or bicycles without a helmet? According to the National Institute of Neurological Disorders and Stroke (1989), 50,000 children incur head injuries in bicycle accidents every year—and 400 of them die. Is the person a rodeo rider? (I tested a person with serious cumulative damage from being thrown many times.) Having the person describe his or her general life-style will allow you to use your judgment about organic potential.

CHILD ABUSE

Be sure to ask about a history of child abuse. It is an unfortunate fact that 64% of all head injuries in infants result from child abuse (National Institute of Neurological Disorders and Stroke, 1989). Brain damage can result from direct blows to the head, but are equally likely to result from the infant being shaken by an angry person. When a child is severely shaken, the brain twists around the brain stem and slams back and forth against the skull. I do not think I need to decribe to you the damage that can be done under these circumstances. The damage may not be apparent at the time of the abuse. The damage may be in the form of tearing apart the connections within the brain (called axonal shearing). Specific damage may occur but not be readily apparent because the skill controlled by that part of the brain is not yet needed. The damage may become apparent when the child starts school and cannot read well or has trouble with math.

Poor diet in infancy and early childhood can result in permanent brain impairment. This point applies to all infants and young children who were nutritionally deprived, intentionally or not.

THE ONUS IS ON YOU

As I am reasonably sure many of you have already learned in your mental health practice, histories can be notoriously inaccurate. We have all been embarrassed when some point comes out later that we should have known. Although the client may have purposely withheld information, more often than not it was something the client simply forget or did not consider important enough to mention. The onus, then, is on you to be sure you ask the right questions and follow up any possible leads. For example, a comment that a client likes to go out and drink on weekends should be followed up by asking the usual questions, but also with, "Do you ever get into fights?" The client who reports a short stay in the hospital after being unconscious from a fall and says, "The doctor said everything was OK," should be asked, "Did you have a CT scan and did you go back for a follow-up?" The client who says, "I've had all kinds of jobs" should be pressed to describe them.

Whatever a client reports, be sensitive to the possibility that further inquiry may be necessary. Do not accept client assurances that it was "nothing" or that everything turned out fine. Find out to your own satisfaction how matters turned out or if a situation was serious. As you would in any interview situation, but especially here, be careful not to lead the client by intimation that there should have been some sort of change or some kind of predictable effect. Be careful that the client does not pick up that you are expecting certain effects or that you are attempting to establish a relationship between symptom onset and some event. Use the standard guideline of asking general questions first, and becoming more specific as the situation dictates.

5 SCREENING: PHYSICAL SIGNS

If asked about the physical signs of brain impairment, the majority of people would most likely describe such symptoms as blurred vision, headaches, dizziness, vomiting, or motor difficulties such as weakness, poor coordination, and problems of balance. Although these signs are definitely reasons for concern, to screen psychiatric patients for possible brain dysfunction we in the mental health field must consider a larger list of symptoms. As Patton and Sheppard (1956) noted, meningiomas (a type of brain tumor) often produce only *psychiatric* symptoms. Soniat (1951) wrote that the medically common triad of headache, vomiting, and papilledema (swelling at the back of the eye where the optic nerve enters the eyeball) are *late* signs of brain tumors, not early signs. Weinberger (1984) noted that, "[C]lassical neurological manifestations of brain disease such as headache, visual symptoms, alterations in motor and sensory functions, and seizures rarely lead directly to psychiatric consultation" (p. 1521). By the time clients show the signs Soniat and Weinberger discussed, the clients are likely to be under medical care or to be seeking it. If any of the classic signs are present, a neurological referral is definitely in order, but their absence does not mean the client is free of neurological involvement.

The physical signs to be presented in this chapter are those that any nonmedical person should be able to recognize. Some of these signs are directly observable by the interviewer, whereas other signs will not become evident without inquiry. Because of the specialized skills and equipment needed, this chapter will not discuss signs that are not readily apparent (such as papilledema, mentioned previously). However, I will caution you to read any medical reports for conditions suggesting the possibility of brain problems, even if the report does not specifically note neurological involvement. For example the report may note a history of cancer, frequent headaches, or complaints of coordination problems.

As an example of the need for careful reading of previous material, a few years ago I completed a vocational placement assessment on an 18-year-old client who, at the time of referral, was not reported to have any neurological problems. Further, none of the previous reports mentioned anything about brain problems. Prior to seeing the client I read through the previous reports. Somewhere in one of the reports a drug was mentioned that I recognized to be an anticonvulsant medication (but there was no mention of seizures). When I saw the client, he acknowledged that he had had grand mal seizures for several years.

When you read any available material about your clients, look for indications of possible brain involvement, whether or not it was formally discussed. Essentially, look for the medical signs that were presented in the previous chapter. Do not assume past mental health or physical examinations necessarily detected a physical problem. The research in Chapter 2 clearly showed that supposing problems were detected is not a warranted assumption.

The following list of physical signs is not presented in any particular order of importance. Each factor must be assessed. As you consider each factor, do so in your usual interviewing style. The physical signs presented here do not require that you actually try to examine a client's physical condition. If the situation is at a point that such an examination is required, it has become a medical matter. If any physical signs are evident, be sure to ascertain when they began, under what circumstances they appeared, and whether or not they are improving, are stable, or are getting worse.

PHYSICAL SIGNS TO NOTE

General Physical Appearance

Notice if the person is as clean and well-groomed as would be expected. Is clothing worn in the appropriate manner, and is it correctly fastened? Is make-up on in a generally orderly manner? Although this may sound a bit farfetched, think about it. Impairments in coordination or vision may account for difficulties in these areas. Problems in grooming and hygiene may reflect a lack of concern about social standards (a not uncommon effect of frontal lobe involvement). Obviously, you must consider occupation, socialization, and other relevant factors in deciding what is or is not appropriate. Use your judgment. It would certainly be warranted, for example, to be concerned about a highly educated, upper middle class professional who comes in wearing dirty clothing, with shirt or blouse misbuttoned, and personal hygiene obviously lacking. Although these could be signs of serious depression, they may also be signs of a brain disorder.

As you talk and listen to the client, carefully observe the person's face and head for scars and indentions that may indicate a head injury or previous neurosurgery. Do not hesitate to ask the person how the scars or indentions were acquired. If the person claims not to know how the marks occurred, do not assume he or she is being purposefully evasive. In a dramatic case I have described elsewhere (Holmes, 1988), I tested a man with an obvious scar running across the top of his head from temple to temple. I knew from the medical record that he had undergone surgery just 3 weeks prior to my seeing him. At the first testing he told me he had fallen in the shower; hence, the scar. Five weeks later he told me that he had fallen on the sidewalk. Even when I presented the specific details of his case, he continued (quite pleasantly) to deny that he had ever had an injury or brain surgery. In this case, he was demonstrating a not uncommon effect of right frontal damage: failure to recognize the problem (this lack of recognition is called anosognosia). This was a brain effect, not psychological denial. Given this example, it is likely you are wondering how you are ever supposed to know for sure if a client is aware of the problem or is reporting it accurately. As I have noted before, you will have to use your clinical judgment, and, when in doubt, make a referral.

In the case of scars only, you need to know the details of how they were acquired. The intent here is to establish if there is a possibility of brain injury. If a scar resulted from a superficial wound, there is no reason for concern, but if the scar resulted from the client hitting his or her head on the dashboard in an automobile accident, concern is obviously warranted. In the case of indentions in the skull, if the client's report and the medical records establish no explanation, refer the person for a medical examination. It is possible that he or she incurred an injury that was not recognized.

Asymmetry

The left and right sides of the human body are not precise mirror images of each other but they should be roughly symmetrical in appearance, function, and strength. A lack of symmetry is important because it may indicate nerve damage, brain damage, or impaired muscle control (which may reflect either of the first two). Both arms and legs should move the same. One of the factors assessed in a neuropsychological examination is whether or not the right and left sides function in close agreement with each other.

Pay attention to the person's face while he or she watches you, talks, smiles, laughs, or cries. The left and right sides should be roughly symmetrical. Does one side sag relative to the other, either as a whole or in part (e.g., eyelids or mouth)? Asymmetry does not necessarily indicate a problem that warrants great concern, but it does indicate a need for further inquiry. Inquiry may reveal, for example, that a childhood accident resulted in some muscle damage (but no brain injury), or that a nerve was damaged at birth, thus accounting for the lack of symmetry.

While you are observing the face, is any drooling apparent? This is a common symptom of Parkinson's disease, related to decreased swallowing. Is the person's face animated, or is it masklike and expressionless? Realizing that this sounds like depression, the difference is that in brain disorders there is less likelihood of classical depressive signs. (Of course classic signs of depression are no guarantee that organicity is not involved.)

Eyes

This refers to the physical aspects of the eyes, not to the process of vision. Vision will be discussed in a separate section. As you interact with the client, watch his or her eyes for normal movement. Do both eyes track you when you move? Do the eyes move in unison? Is there any unusual jerking of the eyes (up and down, back and forth)? Look to see if the pupils are equal in size and if they accommodate to light. The pupils should get smaller when exposed to light and should get larger when the light dims. I am sure a number of you are already familiar with some of these signs as you have worked with substance abusers.

Gait

Notice how the person walks. Walking should be smooth, balanced, and coordinated. Does she or he hesitate or have difficulty getting started? Are the feet lifted off the floor in the usual manner? Check to see if the person is shuffling, dragging a foot, tends to veer off to one side while walking, or seems unsteady. Does the person walk as quickly as one would expect for a person of that age? If there are any difficulties in walking, ask about them. Such difficulties can result from many non-brain causes, and the person may be quite aware of them (e.g., as a result of an accident in which a leg was injured).

Weakness

Does the person exhibit the amount of strength one would expect for a person of that age and general physical condition? For example, is getting out of the chair a difficult task? Is there trouble holding test items, or pencils? If the person shakes your hand, is the grip appropriate? Weakness on only one side is especially noteworthy. For example, holding a block with the right hand may be normal, but from the left hand the block is dropped. Equalized weakness on both sides may indicate brain problems, but may also reflect other medical conditions. One-sided weakness is certainly a sign requiring further examination.

Impaired Coordination

This topic has been partially addressed in previous sections, but there is more. Are physical movements executed in the smooth, continuous patterns we would expect of a person with normal muscle coordination? The presence of jerking movements or uncontrolled motions of the whole body or parts of the body should be a matter of concern. Are movements carried out in the proper sequence to complete an act? When the person reaches for something, is he or she consistently slightly off target? In walking, do the arms swing freely? Does the person exhibit problems of balance? Notice if the person has to steady one hand with the other. You may note that the person holds objects, such as a glass or cup, with both hands when most people would use one hand.

Fluidity of Movement

When the person moves does she or he exhibit the fluidity of movement one would expect, or does the person appear rigid in motion and in posture? Anyone who has worked with patients on some of the antipsychotic medications has seen this rigidity. This is a good example of why knowledge of medications is so important. Are the person's movements obviously slow and deliberate, as if he or she has to think out each aspect of the act?

Tremors and Tics

Watch the person for tremors and tics, either gross (coarse) or fine. The particular conditions under which the person demonstrates a tremor can be diagnostically significant, but a discussion of them is beyond the scope of this book. Although the presence of tremors does not necessarily indicate a serious problem (there is a condition known as familial tremor, in which fine tremors occur but no brain impairment can be found), it must be investigated. Tics are often considered to be learned anxiety reducers, but they can also be indications of organic problems. Perhaps one of the better known examples of this is Tourette's disorder, in which facial grimacing is not uncommon.

Speech

Although it is not easy to separate the physical from the cognitive aspects of speech, the emphasis in this section is on the physical execution of speech. The cognitive aspects will be discussed in Chapter 6. Because the production of speech involves many areas of the brain, impaired speech can reflect a number of different dysfunctions.

Listen to articulation. The words should be clearly pronounced and enunciated. Slurred speech should raise your suspicion. Does speech begin with ease or does the person seem to labor to form sounds and to speak? Speech should flow in an even, consistent pattern. Does the person speak in bursts of sounds? Prosody refers to the rhythm and melody of speech, that is, *how* it sounds, irrespective of *what* is being said. Does the person's speech reflect normal intonation, rhythm, and melody or does it sound mechanical or flat? Listen especially for slow, scanning speech. Although the person may make perfect sense in what is said, speech sounds as if it is being played at slow speed and as if the person is having to make an unusual effort to pick and pronounce each word.

Aphasia refers to brain-based difficulties in language (Strub & Black, 1988). This usually refers to speech but also includes problems in written or sign communication. There are many forms of aphasia, and a listing of them is not necessary. Aphasias are important in the screening process because they can be confused with thought disorder. Two examples should help understand this. In one type, Broca's aphasia, the person speaks in a halting manner reminiscent of reading a telegram (hence, this is called telegraphic speech). Words are omitted, there is commonly an absence of complete sentences, and grammatical rules are violated. In Wernicke's aphasia, speech is fluent but makes little or no sense to the listener, thus sounding very psychotic-like. To the trained person there are ways to distinguish aphasias from each other (e.g., whether or not the person comprehends others' speech), but such techniques are not needed here.

The important point to remember here is that impaired communication does not necessarily reflect a psychotic condition. In general, the aphasic person will be notable by the *absence* of other psychotic diagnostic signs. At this point it may occur to you that when someone's speech becomes impaired medical attention will certainly be sought. Clearly this is not the case, especially if the person who suffers the damage does not show other obvious physical signs of brain dysfunction.

Vision

This is a factor that you will learn through inquiry. The process of vision is a fascinating one, and some of the problems that can occur in the visual system sound more like science fiction than reality. Just in the last several years a great deal of new information has been uncovered about this topic, but a detailed discussion of these results is not necessary to the task of screening. The eyes are extensions of the brain; therefore, visual difficulties can be indicators of brain dysfunction.

Areas of concern here include complaints of blurred or distorted vision (items appearing smaller or larger than they are, or seeming to be unusually close or far away). Does the person not see items in certain parts of the visual field? In looking at something, does the person appear not to see part of it? For example, does he or she start reading in the middle of the line, or does he or she describe only half of a picture? Although it may seem impossible for a person to have these kinds of visual difficulties and not know it, I assure you it is quite possible. The brain has a remarkable ability to fill in the gaps of perception or to justify what is or is not seen.

Headaches

Although this was addressed in the previous chapter, more discussion is needed, as it is not uncommon for a client to complain of headaches. Anyone who complains of persistent headaches and has not obtained a medical evaluation of them must be referred. It goes without saying that the client's self-diagnosis does not count. It is commonly believed that headaches from a brain disorder are excruciating, unrelenting, and unique. Although this is typically true of headaches due to certain conditions (e.g., meningitis or encephalitis), it is not true of other brain-related headaches. Headaches from brain tumors, for example, can present symptoms ranging from tolerable to unbearable (Adams & Victor, 1985).

The critical point with headaches is whether or not a medical evaluation has been obtained. Most headaches are as innocuous as we think they are. They do not portend serious brain problems, or any other serious problem for that matter. Even if you are familiar with the different types of headaches and their characteristic signs, this is a matter too important not to refer the person for a neurological examination. Never assume a psychogenic cause for persistent headaches, even if the person appears to have every psychological reason in the world to justify them.

Seizures/Convulsions

This is a condition whose symptoms you are unlikely to actually observe. You will probably hear about it from the client, his or her relatives, or medical records. Seizure disorders (or convulsive disorders) come in a wide variety of forms. Not surprisingly, the obvious forms— those involving loss of consciousness and dramatic muscle movements (e.g., what is commonly called grand mal seizures)—are usually detected quickly and receive medical attention. Other forms of seizures are not obvious and may go undetected by both the client and others.

Although different authors suggest slightly different ages of onset, any person 30 years or older who has a seizure for the first time absolutely must be referred to a neurologist. This is not optional. I assessed a 31-year-old man for vocational training (not neuropsychologically) who had recently begun to have generalized tonic-clonic (grand mal) seizures, with no history of epilepsy or head injury. The person's physician prescribed an anticonvulsant medication but, according to the client, decided to "watch the problem" for a while before doing anything else. There is no doubt this man should have been referred to a neurologist (this was addressed).

Two specific types of seizures must be discussed because they are not readily apparent, and the symptoms are likely to lead to mental health consultation. Absence seizures (or petit mal, as they are commonly known) are marked by brief periods of inattention but no loss of consciousness. The person just seems to stare off into space for a brief time (usually a few seconds) and is unaware of his or her environment during the seizure. Not realizing the client is having seizures, people who know the client will describe him or her as distracted, inattentive, and forgetful. The client *seems* forgetful because whatever is said or done by others during the time of the seizure is not registered in memory. These seizures may occur many times per day. The similarity between this disorder and certain aspects of attention deficit disorders is obvious.

The second type of seizure disorder, complex partial seizure disorder (also called psychomotor or temporal lobe epilepsy), is characterized by the person carrying on activities but having no recollection of them. There is no loss of consciousness. The seizures may last for a few minutes to hours, during which the person is clearly not himself or herself. Those who know the person can tell something is not right, but the lack of obvious physical signs leads to the assumption that the problem is psychological. Whether or not the person having the seizure can carry out organized activities is a matter of some debate. The first Halstead-Reitan battery I administered was to a truck driver whose last memory prior to the seizure was that he was nearing his destination (a large city). His next memory was of being several hundred miles away from the city and having no idea how he got there. He had been injured in an accident a few years before, but a seizure disorder was not diagnosed at the time. The diagnosis of complex partial seizure disorder at the time I saw the man was made by the neurology department.

Not surprisingly, complex partial seizures are likely to be misdiagnosed as dissociative states or psychotic conditions. In fact, psychotic-like symptoms may occur during these seizures; for example, delusional episodes, hallucinations, or typical signs of a thought disorder. A helpful distinguishing sign is that the person is "psychotic" on a sporadic basis, showing no such signs in between seizures.

Be sure to ask the client (or an informed other) about distortions of perception, altered body image, and altered states of consciousness because these conditions are common with temporal lobe seizures (but not restricted exclusively to them). "Altered states of consciousness" is vaguely defined and is usually described as a peculiar feeling, or of not being oneself.

There is a condition called pseudoseizures. In these cases the person, usually diagnosed as a conversion disorder, appears to have a seizure but in reality is neurologically intact. Although there are some signs to help differentiate pseudoseizures from actual seizures, you must always assume the seizures are genuine. A neurologist must decide this one.

Incontinence

Onset of incontinence after the person has achieved bladder control must be immediately referred. Although this usually applies to an adult, it could also apply to an older child. Incontinence may come from a number of nonbrain causes, but, regardless of cause, medical examination is needed. The reason incontinence is of special concern is that it may be an indication of frontal lobe involvement. Just as with seizure onset in an adult, incontinence offers no option: The client must be referred.

The previous list covers the most common types of physical symptoms you will see. The more you read in this area, the more subtle signs you will pick up. In his book on screening for organicity, Taylor (1990), presented a good description of physical conditions and discussed some of these more subtle signs.

Before leaving this section, it is important to note that a brain-impaired person may have rather obvious symptoms, yet be unaware of them. Self-awareness is a brain function—and it can be impaired just as any other function can be impaired. The brain-impaired person who is not aware of a rather glaring deficit (physical or mental) is not necessarily being "defensive" and denying it. In other cases, the deficiency may have come on slowly enough that the brain has been able to compensate for it. For example, slow-growing tumors usually present less dramatic symptoms than fast-growing ones.

INTEGRATING MATERIAL

Having presented in this chapter and the previous one a number of signs of possible organic involvement, it is time to discuss the process of integration of material. There is nothing here different from what you would use in any other diagnostic procedure. The more signs one has of a disorder, the more likely the clinician is to entertain it as a diagnosis.

In the previous chapter, pertinent indicators from the client's history were presented. Any one of them may be sufficient to warrant a referral. The historical factors, however, take on even greater meaning if any of the factors in this chapter are applicable. Inversely, if signs from the present chapter are accompanied by historical indicators, the chances of organic involvement increase. The more indicators that apply, the greater the likelihood of a brain disorder. This process of integration of material carries on into the next chapter, which presents the psychological (cognitive) indicators of possible organicity.

6 SCREENING: PSYCHOLOGICAL/ COGNITIVE SIGNS

Screening based on psychological/cognitive factors is very difficult because of the overlap between functional and organic disorders. With only an occasional exception, the symptoms described in this chapter could easily apply to either functional or organic problems. The same symptom may indicate an organic problem in one case and a functional disorder in another. This is unavoidable, and it does make the task frustrating and difficult. It would be ideal if there were a clear-cut set of organic-only psychological/cognitive symptoms, but this is not the case. There is, then, ambiguity, confusion, and overlap. Even the most highly trained professional will have times when the situation is anything but clear.

The question I am sure you will ask at some point is, "How am I supposed to know if the person's psychological/cognitive symptoms are functional or organic?" Perfect differentiation is not possible, but there are some guidelines that can be helpful in deciding if symptoms warrant further investigation.

GENERAL GUIDELINES FOR ORGANIC VERSUS FUNCTIONAL DISORDERS

Onset

As you know from your clinical practice, most psychiatric problems have certain conditions related to onset. Some disorders require a precipitating event, others usually emerge at or before a certain age, and some develop endogenously. As I have noted previously, the mental health field's understanding of psychological problems, especially in terms of causes, is incomplete. The field is not yet able to state precise, invariant conditions that precede mental illness. However, we can only work with the best available knowledge. Given this caveat, ask if the onset of symptoms follows the expected pattern.

Any deviation from the expected should raise suspicion. For example, concern is warranted if a 50-year-old man shows signs of psychosis for the first time. Onset of antisocial personality traits in a 25-year-old client with no history of such behavior dating back to the teen years and younger should cause suspicion. Recent onset of writing problems in a previously successful high school student is noteworthy. It is certainly possible that a psychological problem existed for a considerable time before it was diagnosed; therefore, recent onset is not an accurate description. (I am assuming in this book that recent onset means recent onset, not recent diagnosis of a long-standing problem.)

Be especially aware of the onset of symptoms following a situation that could have resulted in brain impairment. For example, questions should be raised about a person seeking psychiatric help several months after a serious automobile accident, even if she or he was pronounced well at the time. We should wonder about a child whose parents report him or her as being less attentive than before, and who note that the child had "just a concussion" from a fall. If the onset of symptoms follows a new medication or a change in dosage, further investigation is warranted. Without repeating all the material in Chapter 4, always consider the possibility of a correlation between some physical event and the onset of symptoms.

Completeness of Symptom Picture

Anyone who has worked in the mental health field expects marked individual differences across people with the same diagnosis. Not all the specific criteria have to be present for a diagnosis to describe a person. On the other hand, people who share a common psychiatric diagnosis will have certain important similarities to each other. For the screening process, even though we do not expect identical descriptions of every client in a diagnostic category, there should be a fairly complete complement of the significant diagnostic signs.

If your client only partially fits the expected diagnostic pattern, questions should be raised. For example, the presence of only hallucinations should be a warning signal, especially if they are visual. This reflects the observation that whereas auditory hallucinations are common among the functional psychoses (especially schizophrenia), visual hallucinations are often related to organic psychoses. The typical functional psychosis would simply not have such a discrete, isolated symptom picture. Where are the thought disorder, the delusions, or the affective symptoms? A person who presents with conversion or dissociative symptoms but without the usual anxiety (neurotic) make-up should be assessed very carefully. An individual with psychotic symptoms whose extended family has absolutely no history of such problems must be interpreted carefully. You are looking for a close fit between what the person is *expected* to show and what the person *does* show. Of course, discrepancies between what *should be* and what *is* do not ensure the presence of an organic problem. We cannot expect a perfect fit, but the fit should not have glaring inconsistencies.

Poor Health

A client in poor health for any reason must be diagnosed very carefully, even if the problem is not specifically a neurological one. As you read in Chapter 2, there are many possibilities for physical illness to mimic or coexist with a psychiatric one. If the person has a physical illness, consider its possible interaction with psychiatric conditions. If the illness is not related to psychiatric symptoms, perhaps the person's medications are producing psychiatric effects. Regardless of the specific illness, it cannot be dismissed without careful consideration.

These are guidelines, not rules. You know that an organic disorder may almost perfectly mimic a psychogenic one. While acknowledging that screening for organicity does not involve clear-cut criteria, the ambiguity does not excuse us from the task.

PSYCHOLOGICAL/COGNITIVE SYMPTOMS

The following factors are essentially part of, or minor additions to, the standard mental status examination. In some cases deciding if they are physically based or psychogenic requires special inquiry (e.g., separating a memory deficit from an attention problem), but the clinical skills you already possess will allow this with no great difficulty.

Memory

The study of memory is a rapidly growing area, and the classification of memory and its disorders is changing in light of new research. Experts in the field of memory do not agree on terminology and classification; therefore, you may encounter different terms for the same type of memory. Although classification and terminology are in flux, one fact is beyond dispute: Memory is not a unitary phenomenon.

There are many types of memory. We are all familiar with the distinction between recent and long-term memory. However, there are also verbal or semantic memory (words), spatial memory (the location of items), episodic memory (events), and figural memory (items such as shapes), to name a few. It is not necessary that you know the names of all the different types of memory to be able to assess them. All that is required is that you expand your assessment beyond verbal and episodic memory and inquire about difficulties remembering *anything*. Let the client's replies direct your questions to get as precise a description as possible of the problem.

Genuine memory impairment is not a typical symptom of psychiatric disorders, but it is an extremely common symptom of brain impairment. Memory for recent events is usually the first to be affected, with memory being lost in reverse order of how it was acquired (i.e., earliest memories are the last to be lost). However, damage to different areas of the brain may affect different types of memory. Memory loss can be general or quite specific.

You must establish that the client has a true memory deficit. Problems with attention are often confused with memory difficulties. Depressed, anxious, thought-disordered, or distracted clients may give the appearance of a memory problem when, in fact, the problem is one of inattention. In these clients, material may not be recalled but memory is fine. The problem is that the material never got into memory because the person was not paying attention. Complaints of memory loss are common in neurologically intact depressed older persons. Because of the depression, the people do not pay attention to their surroundings, and material never gets registered in memory. Failure to recall something is then erroneously interpreted as memory loss. Because the person *seems* to be suffering dementia, this is called pseudodementia.

Memory impairment must be considered in light of what you would reasonably expect from a particular client, considering her or his overall intellectual functioning. If you are unsure as to how to differentiate a genuine memory loss from psychological conditions, the solution is to refer the person for testing. The fact that the question has been raised is sufficient reason to seek clarification.

Disorientation

Of course, disorientation for time, place, and person are classic signs of the psychoses, especially schizophrenia. They may also be signs of organic involvement. One point that is likely to help differentiate functional from organically based disorientation is that the person with a brain disorder is not likely to show the full symptom picture of a psychotic disorder.

There is another type of disorientation, however, that is not common among psychiatric disorders: spatial disorientation. This type of disorientation refers to the inability to remain oriented within the environment in terms of location, direction, and the relationship of items or locations in relation to each other. The spatially disoriented person turns directions around, gets lost easily in a familiar environment, or goes to the wrong place. Even after repeated instruction and practice, the difficulty continues. He or she may have great difficulty telling left from right. Items may be placed on a shelf in a precarious position. A cup may be missed when trying to pour something in it. There may be misses or near-misses when the person reaches for something.

Spatial disorientation is not a memory problem. It reflects impairment to certain areas of the brain (commonly, right parietal). This is why repeated instruction is not likely to help. Instruction cannot make the brain work correctly again. This is not to say that the situation is hopeless. Compensatory skills can be learned or changes in the environment may help (e.g., making living arrangements less complex).

Neurologically intact people differ considerably in spatial skills, as they do with any brain function. Some people have a remarkable capacity to maintain direction, whereas others have never been especially good at it. This does not mean that the less able person has a brain problem. It simply means that spatial skills are not one of her or his strong points. Given this, if a person has never been very good at directions or any other spatial skill, there is less reason to be concerned— with two stipulations. First, make sure that there is no history of brain injury. Having "always been this way" may reflect an early injury or illness. The second stipulation is that the lack of spatial skills does not create any serious problems. Disorientation resulting in serious problems such as getting lost if the route home is slightly altered should be referred, irrespective of how long the person has had it.

Comprehension

Comprehension refers to a person's ability to understand communications and directions, considering the person's intellectual functioning, education, and experiences. In other words, comprehension must be considered in the context of overall intellectual abilities. Using these factors as a baseline allows us to determine if comprehension is what it should be. Knowing that a person is a college graduate allows the assumption that he or she should understand simple instructions. Knowing that a person has been an effective therapist allows some estimate of what may be expected of her or him. Essentially, we are asking if the person understands what he or she should understand, and if there has been any decline in comprehension level relative to past performance.

Genuinely impaired comprehension is not characteristic of psychogenic disorders. The thought-disordered, anxious, depressed, or uncooperative client may not follow directions well or may not seem to understand your conversation, but is it a problem of comprehension? In these cases, inattention, impaired thought processes, or purposeful lack of cooperation might better explain the situation.

In assessing comprehension, in addition to the points already mentioned, be sure the client *really* understands conversations or directions. Do not categorically accept his or her word for it. Ask the client to paraphrase what was just discussed, or have the person do something to show that directions were understood. Note at what level comprehension occurs. Is comprehension intact when conversations and directions are kept simple, yet fails when the interaction becomes more complex? Keep the discussion within the expected level for that client in assessing what is simple and complex.

Confabulation

Confabulation has several meanings. It may refer to the process of carrying on a conversation, a process of elaboration, or the fabricating of details to cover gaps in memory. The last meaning will be used in this discussion. In other words, confabulation refers to a person covering a memory problem by reporting accounts and details that, in fact, never happened.

Although I have seen confabulation in other brain problems (e.g., tumor), Korsakoff syndrome is a dramatic example. This syndrome is associated with a vitamin B-1 deficiency related to excessive consumption of alcohol. The person suffers a severe memory loss but tends to cover it by offering plausible but false (confabulated) details. The person does not appear to be consciously distorting or having to work at creating the details. To the contrary, the words come out quickly with no apparent forethought. The accounts are often quite believable, with specific details being provided; therefore, you would have little reason to question the person. For example, one person discussed in specific detail a phone call that never happened (I found this out when the other person indicated no such call had occurred).

The assessment of confabulation is easy if the details are known to be false. For example, you know the person has not left the hospital for the last few days, yet she or he discusses, in detail, a family picnic at home last evening. Assessing confabulation requires that you know the truth, but what about circumstances when this is not possible? First, listen for differing details in repeated descriptions. Recalling that the basis for confabulation is a memory deficit, it is not likely that an account given a few hours or days ago will be remembered. Second, discussion with other staff members, family, or friends, or a check of available records may be helpful to establish facts and to see if others have also suspected confabulation.

If confabulation sounds psychotic, it is not. Confabulated accounts are likely to be clear, common, coherent, and not bizarre (in contrast to delusions, which are notable by their psychotic qualities). Confabulation is not a common sign of psychiatric problems. Its presence warrants further investigation.

Mental Processing

A common result of brain impairment is a slowing in the speed of mental processing. The person's responses indicate that she or he understands, but it takes longer for the information to get through the brain. Client thoughts are usually expressed clearly, but only after a delay. Speech itself may or may not be slowed. Mental processing is directly analogous to the operations of a slow computer and a fast one. Both computers accurately process identical amounts of material but one is much slower than the other. So it is with mental processing: The task gets done but it takes somewhat longer than it should. Slowing of mental processing is often obvious in a person who has sustained a severe brain injury.

As was true with memory and comprehension, how quickly a person should process material must be assessed in light of what is reasonable to expect, considering the person's intellectual functioning and experiences. One could reasonably expect, for example, a very intelligent person to process information faster than a person in the borderline range. A quick way to assess mental processing speed is to see how fast the client responds to a simple command or request, such as "Put your hand on the table."

Slow mental processing may seem to have a common thread with several psychiatric disorders: psychosis, depression, and obsessive-compulsive disorder. The similarity is superficial. Slow mental processing will usually be clear and rational and will lack psychotic qualities. The absence of depressive symptoms helps separate slow mental processing from depression. The delay in response will not be due to rumination or obsessive attempts to find precise words and meanings.

Alertness/Attention

This is commonly known as level of consciousness. The assessment of alertness begins from the very first contact you have with the client. Does he or she immediately respond to environmental stimuli, such as a greeting or a noise in the hallway? Are actions shown that indicate clear, immediate attention to questions? Does the person remain focused, alert, and responsive as time goes on? Inversely, does the person seem to be in a mental haze, as if drugged? Do you have to keep calling the person back to awareness? Does the person seem focused and alert only when you have had to exert considerable effort to arouse him or her? Do only the most vivid stimuli command the person's attention, with less intense ones being allowed to slip away unnoticed? Does the person seem to have to exert considerable effort just to remain focused?

I saw a client at the request of a psychiatrist who already suspected brain dysfunction. The man, 80 years old, was cleanly and neatly dressed, sitting on the edge of his hospital bed. He seemed unaware of my entrance but was not startled by my introduction. If I asked a question, he responded understandably and coherently but immediately fell back into mental passivity. He would respond when spoken to but would again retreat, for all intents and purposes as if I was not there. He was not uncooperative; to the contrary, he was friendly and polite. A CT scan revealed cortical atrophy.

During my neuropsychology training I was taught the importance of going to the ward to get a client, even if she or he was quite capable of getting to the neuropsychology office unassisted. Going to the ward and interrupting whatever was going on (including napping) offered the chance to see how quickly the client could orient to the new situation (as well as providing a chance to observe any number of other functions, such as physical skills and spatial orientation on the client's part).

Confusion

Confusion means the same thing here that it would in any other situation: giving inconsistent, contradictory, or changing accounts of events. Although this is not uncommon with brain disorders, it is, of course, common with psychotic individuals. It is the *quality* of the person's verbal performance that is likely to help you decide if the problem is psychotic or organic. Here is a case where an incomplete symptom picture should serve as a warning. If the person is confused but otherwise does not seem psychotic, the possibility of organicity must be considered.

Judgment

Judgment must be assessed in light of a person's intelligence and background. If the person has always exhibited poor judgment or is of lower intellectual capacity, poor judgment is less a worry than if it is a recent symptom. A key word here is "uncharacteristic." Has the person begun, uncharacteristically, to take potentially dangerous risks, such as working with machinery while ignoring safety precautions? The person may cross a busy street without caution, or may make statements or write letters that result in the loss of a job. Financial decisions may lose their once-careful consideration, and comments may be made that offend others. If a person has a history of good judgment, onset of poor judgment must be carefully evaluated even if there are psychological stressors in the person's life.

Planning and Organization

The ability to plan, organize, and follow through with actions is a brain function associated with the very front part of the frontal lobes called the prefrontal or far-frontal area, just above the eyes. All too often, these abilities are not thought of as brain functions. Unfortunately, they are considered some kind of purely psychological functions that are subject to voluntary control. I say *unfortunately* because a person with this brain problem is likely to be greatly misunderstood by other people. Others may see the person as uncooperative, insensitive, inconsiderate, uncaring, or forgetful. It is imperative to know that this is not something the person can make better just by trying harder: It is a brain dysfunction.

Disease or damage affecting the far-frontal region of the brain, whether from direct insult or from more diffuse damage, is likely to result in an impaired ability to plan, organize, and carry out behavior. The person may say something will be done that afternoon, but when you return nothing has happened. The person may discuss definite steps to enroll in a college class, but it never happens. Housework may be left undone or job assignments remain incomplete. Appointments may be missed because the person went somewhere else. A dinner date goes unmet because the affected person went out of town. It is easy to see how this could be mistaken for psychological problems such as passive-aggression or callousness.

As has been true on several points, recent onset is a special reason for concern. If a person has never been especially good at planning and carrying out actions, concern is diminished, but organic possibilities must be still be considered.

Problem Solving

Considering a person's intelligence and past experiences, is she or he able to assess a situation and effect a reasonable solution? Inversely, does the person now seem stymied by problems that once would have been readily addressed? We should be concerned if simple addition now seems difficult or opening a sliding cover on a box appears insurmountable. If the client has special knowledge or skills, problem solving must be considered in light of them. For a professor of mathematics, a simple math skill may be so overlearned that it remains intact in spite of a brain insult. However, the professor will experience difficulties with higher level problems that once would have been easily solved. An electrician may retain certain basic skills, yet be unable to interpret a wiring diagram that once would have been consulted with ease.

Word Finding

Word finding is something about which most of us never give a second thought. It is just a natural part of communicating. The inability to find words that should be *readily* available is not a generally recognized characteristic of psychogenic problems. It is a sign of brain impairment. Word-finding difficulty does not refer to the occasional lapses to which all of us are subject, nor does it refer to problems locating difficult or esoteric words. From time to time we all have had to search for a word that may or may not have eventually come to us. Do not, then, be too quick to conclude word-finding difficulties with a client.

If word finding is a problem, you will detect it because it occurs too frequently and the lost words are usually common enough that they should be readily available to the client. What constitutes a commonly available word depends on the client. A psychologist who cannot come up with an everyday psychological term may have problems. It is not uncommon for a client to circumlocute a word, making it clear that he or she knows what needs to be said, but the word itself remains elusive.

I tested a college-educated man who was trying to come up with the word "rail," referring to railroad tracks. He gave an accurate description of rails' purpose ("The thing the train rides on") and their composition ("Those iron things on the ties"). It was evident that he knew what he wanted to say but he never came up with the word. Although word-finding difficulty is common in Alzheimer's patients (this client's diagnosis), it is not restricted to that disease.

Personality/Social Changes

It is tempting to skip over this topic because it is so difficult to determine if personality changes are organic or psychologically related. However, I cannot possibly ignore this topic because it is virtually synonymous with brain dysfunction. Just as I noted about planning, organizing, and following through with behavior, it must be pointed out that personality/social functions are controlled by the brain, specifically the far-frontal region of the frontal lobes.

Virtually all people who incur some kind of brain impairment will show personality and social changes. Some changes may be subtle, thereby avoiding detection. Other changes will be dramatic and obvious. Unfortunately for the mental health professional's screening task, there is no particular pattern of personality changes I can describe. Literally anything is possible. The person may become more of something or less of something. Premorbid characteristics may be exaggerated or lessened. The changes may be for the better or for the worse. It is not possible to describe what you should expect; all changes are possible.

To help decide if personality/social changes are possibly brain related, consider a number of points. First, if the person is older (perhaps 50+) you should automatically be wary of personality changes. Given that this is a time when social and personal stresses may be part of the client's life, it is easy to assume the changes are a reaction to stress, but be careful. Second, did the changes occur after some event such as an accident, illness, or change in medication? The relationship between a biological factor and personality/social changes is not always easy to detect because some changes come on gradually.

Third, if there are significant psychological factors in the person's life, for example, a death, are the kinds of changes consistent with what you would expect under the circumstances? It would be unusual for a previously psychologically stable person to become abusive, paranoid, or callous following a stressor. Be careful about assuming psychological causes, but also be careful not to assume that every personality change reflects a brain disorder.

I wish I could present a foolproof way of telling organic from psychogenic causes of personality changes. Such a way does not exist, and this makes screening difficult. Nonetheless, personality/social changes are so common that they cannot be ignored.

Dementia

Actually, aspects of dementia have been discussed several times already, although they were not identified as such. The term itself refers to a brain impairment resulting in the loss of intellectual abilities (e.g., memory, judgment, attention, or problem solving). True dementia is not a characteristic of psychogenic disorders. Any time a client exhibits a decline in intellectual abilities you must be concerned. You must, of course, determine if the client has really lost intellectual abilities or if psychological problems are simply preventing the abilities from being demonstrated. In addition to the points previously made in this chapter, two more points must be discussed in reference to dementia: intellectual functioning in children, and intellectual loss as a part of aging.

The loss of previously attained academic skills in a child should be immediate reason for referral. One does not lose these abilities unless something is wrong. For example, a child who has been reading at the 3rd-grade level who drops to the 1st-grade level needs further assessment. A child whose writing skills decline is cause for concern. It is most important to emphasize that the concern is over the *loss* of what was once present. The fact that a child's work declines because of increasing difficulty at higher grade levels very likely reflects intellectual limits rather than brain problems. This is not an absolute rule, however, as a child's difficulties may not become apparent until academic tasks in later grades begin to tap the damaged area of the brain. Be alert to this possibility.

Dementia is not a natural function of aging. Dementia is a disease process. The cognitive changes that are a part of the aging process are relatively minor (e.g., it may take a little longer to learn a new task, and spatial memory may show a slight decline). If you have a client with signs of dementia, refer her or him. This is critical, because, of the roughly 50 types of dementia, some are quite treatable and reversible. In Chapter 2, for example, it was noted how frequently the elderly are subject to hematoma, a treatable condition that can create symptoms of dementia.

A Useful Resource

This completes the list of psychological/cognitive screening signs. This is a good time to suggest an excellent book that addresses how a clinician can assess these signs. The book, *The Mental Status Examination in Neurology* (2nd ed.) (Strub & Black, 1985), offers specific concrete, suggestions about the process.

PSYCHIATRIC DIAGNOSES THAT WARRANT SUSPICION

Referring back to the results presented in Chapter 2, several diagnoses stood out as warranting special attention in the screening process. The possibility of brain dysfunction is high enough that the diagnosis itself is sufficient reason to consider referral of the person for further evaluation.

Conversion/Hysterical Disorders

The research on this category clearly places it in a high-risk group. Anyone presenting with conversion, dissociative, or, generally, hysterical symptoms must be considered for referral. This applies both to new diagnoses and to long-term diagnoses that have not been medically assessed. In too many cases, the symptoms are actually the first signs of brain impairment.

Psychosis

This refers to all psychoses. A first-time diagnosis should be referred, but do not rule out future assessments from time to time just to be sure. Psychotic diagnoses are common among people who initially present with psychiatric symptoms but are ultimately shown to have brain disorders.

Substance Abuse

There are two reasons why substance abuse should raise suspicions. First, there is the effect of the substance itself. The ability to damage the brain is well known for some drugs, for example, alcohol. Since many substance abusers are actually polydrug users, it is not unreasonable to expect that the brain has been subjected to various combinations of drugs whose physical effects on the brain are as yet unknown.

The second reason substance abusers should be closely examined is the possibility of brain damage from falls, fights, auto accidents, choking, and dietary deficiencies. Obviously, the longer one has been involved with drugs, the greater the potential for brain damage. Do not assume that a long-term user with organic symptoms will necessarily have seen a physician.

I tested a man in his mid-40s who had once owned his own business. He had a long history of severe alcohol dependency. By the time I tested him, he was unable to attain *any* points on four of the subtests on the Wechsler Adult Intelligence Scale—Revised. This kind of impairment certainly had not developed overnight, yet the client had not yet seen a neurologist.

Children

It would be desirable for any child or adolescent to receive a thorough medical examination before entering mental health services. The few articles in Chapter 2 that dealt with children and adolescents showed a high incidence of brain impairment among those in psychiatric care. Be attentive to atypical symptoms among this group.

Elderly

It is apparent that the longer a person has lived, the greater the risk of brain involvement. Because many elderly people are likely to have some kind of health problem(s) and to be on some kind of medication(s), they are at special risk. The single greatest factor that should raise doubts about psychogenic causes in the elderly is a recent onset of psychiatric symptoms. Someone does not live his or her life well adjusted only to lose it due to age. Be careful not to assume a psychogenic cause just because there has been some kind of psychological trauma or significant life change with the person. Change and brain impairment can co-exist.

A REMINDER

In closing this chapter, be reminded that your task is not the precise discrimination of organic versus functional disorders. Your task is to be able to tell who should or should not receive further evaluation. Although any factor in this chapter could be reason for concern, psychological/cognitive impairments take on even greater meaning if there are historical or physical signs that might also cause you to consider organic possibilities.

7   SCREENING: TESTING

At first glance it may seem that the use of psychological tests to assess brain functioning and impairment is inappropriate. There is, however, a firm basis for such a procedure. The foundation for neuropsychological testing is that if something is wrong with the brain there will be some kind of detectable effect, either behavioral or psychological. Given that the brain controls behavioral and psychological functioning, assessment is a matter of knowing which brain parts or systems are involved in those functions and then testing for them. Such testing requires extensive knowledge and training, as well as utilization of a battery of tests (some of which are common to all of psychology, some of which are quite specialized). The process of nonmedical testing for brain function is, then, not as farfetched as it might seem at first glance. The research on neuropsychological testing clearly supports its validity. The purpose of this chapter, however, is not to discuss neuropsychological testing in general; rather, it is to examine the possibility of screening for brain dysfunction.

This chapter may be a disappointment for some readers, for there is no such thing as a *simple* screening test for organic involvement. Franzen and Berg (1989) succinctly summarized the present state of simple screening tests by noting, "Over the years, a number of investigators have attempted to identify a single test that will differentiate patients with brain damage from non-brain-damaged individuals. In virtually all instances such attempts have failed and continue to do so. There is a very simple reason for this. One single test cannot possibly tap all aspects of brain functioning" (p. 180). In other words, any single test will at best assess only a limited part of brain functioning. If the brain is impaired in some region other than the one(s) tapped by the test, the dysfunction will go undetected. The reason neuropsychological test batteries can do such a good job of assessing brain dysfunction is that they involve a wide variety of tests and tasks that tap virtually all areas of the brain.

To increase accuracy of diagnosis, the trade-off is increased complexity, time, expense, and training. The administration of a neuropsychological test battery will range from 2 to 3 hours for the Luria Nebraska Neuropsychological Battery (Golden, 1987; Golden, Hammeke, & Purisch, 1980) to 5 to 8 hours for the Halstead-Reitan Neuropsychological Test Battery and allied procedures (Reitan & Davison, 1974). In many cases, additional testing will be necessary, such as detailed testing for aphasia, further personality testing, vocational assessment, or testing for academic performance. This is a significant investment in time, but there is no alternative. There is no short-cut method to assessing the brain accurately. Obviously, the more brain functions that are assessed, the more likely we are to detect a problem if one exists.

Does all of this mean that we should forget about testing as a screening measure? The answer to the question is clearly, "No." Testing can be an effective part of screening, but the testing is going to have to be more involved than the administration of a single, simple test. You or your agency will have to address two questions which only you can answer. First, will all clients be routinely tested or will testing be offered only when there is some reason to suspect brain impairment (recalling that the previous three chapters of this book offered screening indicators that did not involve testing)? Second, how much time can be devoted to the testing? The other side of these questions is, How much risk are you willing to take? Assuming valid tests are used, the risk of accurate detection of a brain problem is related to how much testing you do. The fewer tests you use, the less the chance of detecting a problem. When and how much to test must be answered in light of your or your agency's practice. There simply are no hard and fast rules to be offered.

WHAT ABOUT SOME POPULAR SCREENING TESTS?

I am sure you have heard of some quickly administered tests to screen for organic involvement and that their rate of detection is reasonably good. Let us look at some of those tests. Lubin, Larsen, Matarazzo, and Seever (1985) reported the results of an earlier (1982) survey of different mental health settings to see how frequently all types of psychological tests were used. Not surprisingly, the most frequently used tests varied according to the setting (e.g., a psychiatric hospital compared to a facility for the developmentally disabled). However, Lubin et al. gave an overall ranking for the tests by combining the results from the different settings. It is to this overall rating that I will be referring. Of special relevance to the present discussion, it is interesting to note that among the top 20 most commonly used tests, 6 are primarily tests for organicity or are used for that intent in addition to their primary purpose.

The Lubin et al. study found the *Wechsler Adult Intelligence Scale* (original and revised—the revised edition had just come out prior to the study) (Wechsler, 1981) to rank number 2 in frequency of administration, while the *Wechlser Intelligence Scale for Children—Revised* (Wechsler, 1974) ranked number 5. Although these tests were not designed to assess brain impairment, they have been widely studied for such potential. Various techniques, such as comparing the Verbal IQ to the Performance IQ (looking for large differences) and comparing the results of subtests to each other (looking for certain patterns) have been suggested as useful indicators of brain dysfunction.

The *Bender-Gestalt* test (Bender, 1938) was ranked number 3 in the Lubin et al. study. This test involves nine cards, each of which contains a figure. The client views the cards one at a time and then draws the figure immediately from memory, or draws with the card present (there are different ways to administer the test). Certain difficulties in reproducing the figures are thought to indicate brain impairment, for example, rotating the figure when it is drawn. Canter (1966) devised a procedure in which the figures are drawn over dark lines rather than on plain paper.

The 13th-ranked test in the study was the *Wechsler Memory Scale* (Wechsler, 1945), which has since been revised to address criticisms of the original scale (Wechsler, 1987). The new scale assesses a variety of memory functions, such as verbal memory, visual memory, recall of a series of numbers, or learning pairs of words. The *Memory-For-Designs Test* (Graham & Kendall, 1960) was ranked number 15 in frequency. This test consists of 15 cards with a geometric figure on each. The client views the card for a few seconds and then draws the figure from memory. The MFD is obviously similar to the Bender-Gestalt.

The *Revised Visual Retention Test* (Benton, 1974) was ranked 19th.

This test has three comparable forms. It involves the client reproducing figures both immediately and from memory. The 10 cards in each form of the test have from one to several figures. Thus, the Revised Visual Retention Test is considerably more complex than the Bender-Gestalt or the Memory-For-Designs.

Although the *Trail Making Test* (Army Individual Test Battery, 1944) was not included in the top 20 tests in the Lubin et al. article, I should mention it because its screening potential has been explored several times. The Trails (as it is usually called) consists of Trails A and Trails B. Trails A involves the client connecting circled consecutive numbers on a sheet of paper, with time to completion and the number of errors being recorded by the examiner. Trails B involves the client connecting circles again, but the circles alternate between numbers and letters of the alphabet, that is, the client starts at 1, goes to A, then goes to 2, then to B, and so on. Again, time to completion and the number of errors are recorded. Some researchers have supported the Trail Making Test as a screening instrument (Goldstein & Neuringer, 1966; Gordon, 1972, 1978; Mezzich & Moses, 1980), whereas other researchers have failed to find such support (Smith & Boyce, 1962; Watson, Thomas, Anderson, & Felling, 1968). In fact, the Watson et al. article found the complete Halstead-Reitan battery unable to discriminate between organic and schizophrenic patients.

The research on the ability of these seven previously described tests to detect brain impairment remains inconsistent, that is, some studies support their use as screening tests, whereas other studies fail to offer support. For especially good coverage of the topic of screening tests, consult Lezak (1983), Berg, Franzen, and Wedding (1987), and Franzen and Berg (1989). In most cases, the ability of the tests or techniques to detect brain damage (called the "hit rate") is in the 75% to 80% range, sometimes higher. These hit rates may seem impressive, but there is another side to the issue. As Lezak (1983) noted, a signficant problem with these impressive hit rates is that the researchers almost invariably compared results from medically established neurological cases to results from medically normal persons. In other words, the researchers were testing relatively *obvious* brain damage. Under these conditions, almost *any* test would produce an impressive hit rate. I might point out that if a neurological problem is that obvious, giving a screening test is probably rather superfluous.

I realize it could be argued that a few minutes of testing with a single instrument is worth it if the test detects a problem just once in a while.

The danger of this procedure is in concluding that "normal" results mean there is no brain problem. What about the parts of the brain that were not tapped by that instrument? Problems there will not be detected. I administered one of these brief tests to a person several months after removal of a large right frontal tumor. In spite of indisputable evidence of serious neurological damage, the test results were "normal," in fact, perfect. Why? Because the functions measured by the test were controlled by another part of the brain.

Although no single test can serve as an effective screening device, it is important to note that the same test can be quite valuable when it is included as part of a battery of tests. This leads to the logical question of whether or not an effective screening battery can be established.

WHAT ABOUT A SCREENING BATTERY?

A number of researchers have attempted to devise a brief screening battery for organicity. Because detailed discussions of these screening batteries may be found elsewhere (e.g., Berg, Franzen, & Wedding, 1987; Franzen & Berg, 1989), I will not go into any great detail about them. For our purposes, several points should be made. First, the batteries appear to be reasonably effective in accomplishing their task. Second, they range in administration time from less than an hour (Erickson, Calsyn, & Sheupach, 1978) to approximately 2 hours (Barrett, Wheatley, & LaPlant, 1982). Third, there is considerable diversity in the tests used by the various authors. It is interesting to note, however, that all use the Trail Making Test and many use the Aphasia Screening Test (Halstead & Wepman, 1959; Reitan, 1984), a brief aphasia test from the Halstead-Reitan battery. Fourth, because of the nature of the tests, the batteries must be individually administered, that is, a screening program will involve a considerable investment in time.

To go back to the question of the possibility of developing screening batteries, the answer is "yes." Screening batteries can be devised. The questions I posed earlier in this chapter must still be addressed. That is, how much of a risk are you willing to incur, and how much time and expense can be involved in the screening process?

By now you have probably noticed that I am not suggesting any particular screening battery, either from the ones that are available or from my own perspective. I am not suggesting one of my own because to do so competently would require controlled study of the effectiveness of whatever battery I might devise. I am not suggesting one available battery over the others because all present essentially equal results on their effectiveness. The process you will have to follow is to study the individual tests and test batteries and decide within the limits of your practice what is suitable and feasible. Fortunately, there are a number of excellent published sources you may consult. For general coverage of the screening process I suggest Filskov (1984), Berg, Franzen and Wedding (1987), and Lezak (1983). For an emphasis on screening children I suggest Franzen and Berg (1989), Hartlage (1984), and Tupper (1986). By no means is this list exhaustive of the available material, but as you read these you will be directed to other sources. You would undoubtedly find it helpful to consult with a neuropsychologist who could help you tailor a set of tests that would meet any needs particular to your practice.

TESTING AS AN ADJUNCT TO THE INTERVIEW

The Russian neurologist and neuropsychologist A. R. Luria (1902–1977), a name often cited because of his immense contributions to the field, did not favor the idea of a test battery. He favored a test-as-you-go process in which he would devise a task, as needed, to assess a brain function. For example, he might simply have a patient write something, he might have the person name several common objects, or he might have the patient watch him hide something and then later ask where the object was hidden. Such a technique is informative and tremendously efficient because there is no unnecessary testing. However, such an approach is appropriate only in the practice of a very skilled clinician who is intimately familiar with brain functions and how to assess them. Unless you are at this level of skill, a more formal procedure is recommended.

WHERE DOES THIS LEAVE US?

Chapter 7 completes the four chapters on the actual process of screening. The material presented in this chapter leads to two major conclusions. First, no single test can do an adequate job of screening for organicity. Second, screening by means of testing is possible if a battery of tests is used. Although a screening battery involves around an hour or more of individual testing, there is no other way to accomplish the task. Whether or not you want to test everybody who seeks help at your facility is something only you can decide, but I will personally note that because most clients will not have a brain dysfunction, screening everyone with a battery is debatable. Based on the factors presented in Chapters 4, 5, and 6, or perhaps on available test data, you can make a reasonable estimate of who needs to be tested (my personal bias is to test when in doubt). The screening battery can then serve to help you decide who needs to be referred for more comprehensive neuropsychological testing or medical assessment. As I have noted a number of times in this book, no matter how conscientiously we do our job, we will still not attain a 100% accuracy rate. The nature of the field in which we work is such that we are going to miss some cases, but we can minimize the number of missed cases by doing a thorough job of screening.

As I have noted before, and now is a good time to reiterate the point, the possibility of organicity increases as more and more signs point in that direction, from the person's history, psychological signs, or test results, for example. I wish I could offer an empirically based formula that decides the potential for organicity in a person, but such a formula does not exist. Until it does (if ever), we have to base our decisions on our informed judgment.

8 THE REFERRAL PROCESS

The purpose of this chapter is to describe the roles of the professionals to whom you will be making referrals, and to suggest some guidelines about the referral process. If a client you suspect of having a brain disorder does, in fact, have one, you do not want to make referrals that will result in the delay of accurate diagnosis and treatment. Although it is true that in some cases a delay would have no serious health ramifications, it is also true that in other cases a delay could be serious. Before discussing the roles of the various professionals in the field of brain disorders, here are some guidelines about making referrals.

GUIDELINES IN THE REFERRAL PROCESS

The following points are guidelines, not rules. You must use your judgment about the best way to deal with a referral. The exact process must reflect the client's personality and your relationship with him or her and the referral person.

Discussions with the Client or Family

The client has a right to know what is being done with his or her life, and why it is being done. If you feel a referral is needed, the client should be told tactfully but directly. In doing so, explain why you feel the referral is required. That is, explain to the client what has led you to consider the possibility of organicity in her or his case (e.g., a past head injury, a change of medication, symptoms that do not present a clear picture). Avoid any suggestions of medical diagnoses, such as "I am concerned about the possibility of a brain tumor." Also, avoid any suggestions about degree of probability, for example, "There is a good chance it could be Alzheimer's disease." Such statements would be inappropriate and would certainly be premature. I would hate to be responsible for such statements and the stress they are likely to create, only to find out the client is in perfect health.

In general, explain to the client that you simply want to be certain the problem is psychological and that sometimes this entails ruling out possible medical conditions. Assure the client you are not diagnosing or suggesting any condition and that you simply want to provide the most competent service possible. If a client does start worrying or already has hypochondriacal tendencies, you will have to handle it as you would any other similar situation. If you feel a medical referral is needed, you must not let fear of your client's reaction stop you from discussing it. Your tact and clinical skills will be needed. At this point in the screening process there is no cause to alarm or worry the client. Only possibilities are being raised, not facts.

What If the Client Will Not or Cannot Comply?

In some cases, a client simply will not comply with your request. In other cases, a client would be willing to comply with the referral but finances, lack of transportation, or other reasons prevent it. What are you to do? If the person refuses to comply, the only thing you can do is try to convince him or her of the need (I am assuming a court order is not an option). If the problem is one of an inability to comply, referral to a social agency should be initiated if the person is eligible. It comes down to the fact that you cannot make someone follow through with a referral. Although it may be tempting to want to enlist the aid of others to bring about more pressure, be sure you do not violate the client's confidentiality in the process.

Whether or not you will continue seeing a client who will not or cannot comply is something you will have to answer for yourself, in accordance with your profession's code of ethics. If you continue to see a client under these circumstances, I suggest that you take precautions against future legal (civil) action. Because I am not an attorney, it would be inappropriate for me to suggest just how you would accomplish this, but I do recommend finding out.

Communications with the Referral Person

When making the referral it is most helpful for you to state as precisely as possible what symptoms have led you to make the referral. A general statement such as "Does the person have a brain disorder?" does little to direct attention to specific concerns. I suspect all of you have been on the receiving end of a request such as "Does this client have emotional problems?" or, as we often got at the state hospital, "Rule out _____ (fill in the blank)." You know how frustrating it is to be unsure of just what you are supposed to examine, and then have the person who made the referral say, "You didn't answer the question. That isn't what I needed to know."

Of course, if there is enough interviewing, observation, and testing, the problem leading to the referral will eventually be detected, but at what unnecessary expense and time? Even then, without a specific referral question, the report may not address questions of interest to the referring person. In making the referral, then, describe the client's symptoms as accurately as possible. In doing so, avoid the use of neurological terminology, even if you are relatively familiar with it. The effective use of terminology assumes you and the referral person are in precise agreement with each other on the meaning of the terms. Also, do not attempt to diagnose the problem. If an accurate diagnosis can be made, a referral for diagnosis is obviously not necessary.

REFERRAL TO PHYSICIANS

It is recognized that any competent physician can serve as a medical resource. The particular skill of the individual physician is the critical factor in deciding if she or he is an appropriate referral person for your client. A particular family practice physician may be quite knowledgeable about psychiatric medications. A psychiatrist can be quite informed about nonpsychiatric illnesses. A neurologist may be very knowledgeable about internal medicine, and the physiatrist may be expert on brain matters. The point stressed in this chapter is to make the most efficient referral, the one that is most likely to get the information as soon as possible. It is assumed the client will be referred by the initial physician to another specialist, if necessary.

Family Physician

There are three good reasons to keep the family practice physician in mind. First, in many locations a neurologist will simply not be readily available; therefore, a family physician can serve in the initial medical role. Assuming the particular physician is informed about neurological symptoms, he or she can make an initial diagnosis and decision about referring the client to another specialist.

The second reason the family physician is a good referral resource is that the client could be suffering a primary physical problem that is producing brain-related symptoms, for example, diabetes. If this were the case, a thorough medical examination by a neurologist would detect it, but so would an examination by one's family physician.

The third reason for referral to a family physician is that the neurologist may accept referrals only from physicians. In other words, the client must have had an initial medical screening prior to seeing the neurologist.

Psychiatrist

Given that your client is already in mental health treatment or the diagnostic process, a referral to a psychiatrist might seem unnecessary. There is, however, the possibility of a client being treated with the wrong medication or the wrong dosage of a psychiatric drug (noting that for a large number of people psychiatric drugs are prescribed for them by nonpsychiatric physicians). If the initial assessment suggests a possibility of problems related to psychiatric drugs, the psychiatrist may be the most efficient referral source. Also, because the psychiatrist is a physician, she or he may provide the initial medical screening if it is required.

Neurologist

The neurologist diagnoses and medically treats nervous system disorders, in comparison to the neurosurgeon, who specializes in surgical treatment. Your referrals, then, will be to a neurologist. If there is a brain problem, the client should ultimately be under this physician's care, either directly or as a consultant to other professionals.

If the client has previously undiagnosed but definite signs of brain impairment (e.g., seizures) referral to a neurologist is clearly required. If a client has a previously diagnosed neurological disorder, be sure there is a recent neurological examination. Just what constitutes *recent* depends on the nature of the problem, but for anyone seeking psychiatric help, especially for the first time, a neurological examination done a year ago may be too old. The brain can change. Functions can improve or functions can deteriorate over time. New problems can emerge. Let the neurologist decide whether or not a reassessment is necessary.

Physiatrist

A physiatrist is a physician trained in rehabilitation medicine. He or she is then knowledgeable about brain problems as well as other physical problems requiring rehabilitation (e.g., orthopedic injuries). It is most unlikely you would make an initial referral to this physician. However, the physiatrist can be helpful in assessing the effects of medications on the person with a brain disorder. Also, the physiatrist can assist in deciding which medications might be appropriate for the treatment of psychiatric symptoms in a person with a diagnosed brain disorder. Several times I have suggested to physicians that they call a physiatrist for consultation.

REFERRAL TO A NEUROPSYCHOLOGIST

A well-trained neuropsychologist has a great deal to offer in this area. He or she can initially help by providing information on symptoms and their possible relationship to brain disorders. That is, he or she can help decide if your concerns are warranted.

Because of his or her training, a neuropsychologist can help diagnose a brain problem, although this role is declining due to sophisticated brain imaging techniques (e.g., CT scans, Magnetic Resonance Imaging, and very sophisticated forms of EEGs). For example, neuropsychological testing is a helpful way to detect early Alzheimer's disease, so early that structural changes in the brain have not yet occurred to a point they can be seen with current imaging techniques. Certainly, assisting in the differential diagnosis between an organic and a functional problem falls in the realm of neuropsychology.

The neuropsychologist is an excellent consultant to someone working with a client who has a brain dysfunction. To help a person with a brain disorder requires knowledge of the brain and the effects of brain impairment on everyday life. Psychological treatment cannot make the brain work again; therefore, it becomes a matter of engineering the environment or of finding alternative pathways to achieving goals. A neuropsychologist is trained to guide this process.

If there is a diagnosed brain disorder, neuropsychological testing can determine which functions remain and which are impaired. This knowledge is important in helping set realistic expectations and goals for any reason (e.g., educational, vocational, therapeutic).

What about a neuropsychological evaluation if medical examination reveals negative results? There are clearly instances in which a neuropsychological assessment would be warranted, in spite of those medical findings. I have already mentioned early Alzheimer's disease as one which neuropsychological testing may detect before medical signs are apparent. Another example is when a person's medical results show no damage after a mild brain injury (such as a blow to the head). The damage to the brain in such cases may be too diffuse, yet limited in size to show up on a CT or MRI scan (such as diffuse, small areas of damage resulting from axonal shearing). A final example would be in the case of a diagnosis such as attention-deficit hyperactivity disorder or dyslexia, whose physiological basis remains in question. Neuropsychological testing can help determine realistic expectations for the person. If you are unsure as to whether or not a neuropsychological examination would be beneficial, simply check with the neuropsychologist and let him or her decide whether or not to proceed with a comprehensive assessment.

Becoming Tenacious

I knew a man who had a grand mal seizure and was immediately hospitalized for neurological examination. Every test possible was conducted, with no firm reason for the seizures ever being established. The neurologists in this case did not quit until every possibility had been explored. Unfortunately, this is not always the case. Recalling the information in Chapter 2 of this book, it is apparent that a significant number of brain problems are being missed by the professionals who are supposed to be detecting them. Recall the man I discussed earlier who had a recent onset of seizures and the physician was simply "going to watch the problem" for a while.

If the initial referral of your client does not result in conclusive information, suggest the client seek another opinion. Of course, there has to be an end to tenacity. You cannot keep referring a client over and over again just because you suspect a problem and it cannot be found. At some point you must acknowledge the findings. There is no easy answer as to when to stop, but there is a helpful guideline. Tenacity is not necessary if you trust the person or the institution to whom the client was referred. Get to know the professionals in your region, so you can establish a degree of confidence in their decisions.

In ending this chapter, I encourage you to do two things. First, I suggest you err conservatively. That is, refer the client for further assessment if there is a *reasonable* suspicion of brain involvement. It is far preferable to have a suspected brain problem turn out to be healthy than to have a brain disorder go undiagnosed and untreated on the erroneous assumption that the symptoms are purely psychogenic.

The second encouragement is to become more familiar with brain function and its relationship to psychiatric symptoms. There is little reason to doubt that with increasing knowledge we will continue to shift psychiatric disorders from the functional category to the organic one. Helping you become more familiar with brain function is the purpose of the final chapter of this book.

9 DEVELOPING GREATER UNDERSTANDING OF THE BRAIN AND BRAIN FUNCTION

Throughout this book I have repeatedly noted the obvious point that the more you know about the brain and brain function, the better you will be at screening for organicity. The purpose of this chapter is to suggest a program of reading that will help you gain that understanding. In addition to the readings I am suggesting, it would be most helpful to have two additional experiences: attending workshops (seminars, classes, etc.) and actually working with people who have brain disorders.

WORKSHOPS, CLASSES, OR SEMINARS

Attending a well-conducted presentation (seminar, etc.) is a good way to acquire and integrate material by learning from someone who knows the area well. Be selective in choosing these presentations. Be sure they are conducted by people who are trained in some area of the neurological sciences. At present, virtually anyone can present himself or herself as an "expert" on the brain. Take the time to find out if you will be getting your money's worth. Read the credentials of the presenters and see who is sponsoring the meeting. Be sure the meeting is geared to your level of knowledge about the brain and brain function. Attend presentations by different people, not the same ones. This is important because there are differing viewpoints about brain functioning, and you need to be exposed to all of them. No set of guidelines guarantees you will be satisfied, but at least you can avoid wasting your time if the presentation is clearly in question.

Although attending presentations is helpful, you cannot acquire all that you need to know just by attending them. As good as a presentation may be, you must also develop a comprehensive study program and actually work with people who have incurred a brain disorder.

WORKING WITH PEOPLE WHO HAVE
A BRAIN DISORDER

There is no substitute for the actual experience of working with people who have brain impairments. No presentation or book can adequately convey the subtlety of how brain impairments can manifest themselves. I suggest you not be a passive observer. Get actively involved over a sustained period of time. Just how this experience is to be gained will vary. It is usually as simple as offering to become a volunteer in a facility that deals with neurological problems. It may be an apprenticeship-like arrangement, or it may be a formal training program. The important point is to have the experience. As is true in any subject area, the academic side is important, but it must be supplemented with actual experience.

READING ABOUT THE BRAIN

The list of suggested readings I will be presenting is based on my own experiences as I began to read in this area. I found out that this is an area where there are no shortcuts. One must begin at the bottom and work his or her way up in a systematic fashion. As I noted in Chapter 1, I began the study of neuropsychology with virtually no scientific background for it. I had only minimal, introductory science courses, and I taught or had worked in clinical settings. I was, to put it kindly, naive about the brain and how it operates, and I had worked in the mental health field for 16 years by that time.

Based on my experiences, I learned four things that I will share to help make your reading as meaningful as possible. Being guided in your readings, as I was, can help avoid a great deal of confusion and frustration. The following four suggestions will help facilitate your reading.

First, accept the fact that you are in for a considerable investment in time. How much time you spend depends on the level of understanding you plan to attain. Allow plenty of time to accomplish your reading. The farther along you get in your reading, the more technical it will become. Reading may be slower than you hope, and rereading is to be expected. Do not be intimidated by the Latin terminology. It will come in its own time. The reading and rereading will help accomplish this.

Second, the major focus will be on the brain itself, not the rest of the nervous system. Knowing all about the nerves that control movement, for example, or how sensory receptors operate is critical for a neurologist but less so for the nonmedical person. As you read, you will surprise yourself at how much of this you will pick up even without trying, but it only adds to the anxiety when one feels she or he *must* learn all of these details.

Third, focus on gross brain anatomy and how the various parts and systems of the brain affect behavior. Knowledge about neurophysiological and neurochemical matters is critical to people doing basic research on brain function, but you do not need to know a great deal about them. Do not worry, then, if this type of information seems too esoteric.

Fourth, and perhaps of special significance to those of you who are beginning as I did, be aware that the terminology in neuroanatomy is far from agreed-upon by those who use it. Various authors will use different terms to refer to the same brain area. Being naive as I was, I assumed there was a precise set of terms; therefore, when another term turned up I assumed I had missed something. It took a considerable amount of time for me to realize that I already knew about that part of the brain but I had not yet seen that particular term for it.

Sometimes, the different names are similar enough to each other that the reader can at least guess that they are the same (always look it up, though). For example, the Nucleus Basalis of Meynert is also called the Body of Meynert. The terms prefrontal and far-frontal are not as easy to detect as being the same area (those who prefer far-frontal point out that because we are talking about the very front of the brain, prefrontal would be whatever comes before the front). Try the striate bodies compared to the basal ganglia. They refer to the same region. The motor strip is also called the precentral gyrus. Some people speak of a limbic lobe, which becomes confusing when you have just read there are four lobes (frontal, temporal, parietal, occipital). The area of the brain known as the limbic system consists of different brain parts depending on who is defining it. Simply being aware of the discrepancies in terminology helps because it reduces confusion and the feeling of being overwhelmed. I strongly suggest keeping a list of terms that mean the same thing.

SUGGESTED READINGS

The following list of readings is based on my own efforts to gain understanding of the brain. These are books I found especially helpful. There is no accepted "best" reading list, but the following list is a good starting point. If you are already familiar with the literature at one level, begin at the next. Some of the publication dates may seem old, but the books are still appropriate. Some of them are classics.

Level 1: A General Introduction

These books are nontechnical. They will expose you to the general make-up of the brain and to the results of brain impairment.

1. Bloom, F. E., & Lazerson, A. (1988). *Brain, mind, and behavior* (2nd ed.). New York: W. H. Freeman.
2. Ornstein, R., & Thompson, R. F. (1984). *The amazing brain.* Boston: Houghton Mifflin.
3. Luria, A. R. (1968). *The mind of a mnemonist.* New York: Basic Books.
4. Luria, A. R. (1972). *The man with a shattered world.* New York: Basic Books.
5. Sacks, O. (1985). *The man who mistook his wife for a hat and other clinical tales.* New York: Harper & Row.
6. Gardner, H. (1974). *The shattered mind.* New York: Knopf.

Level 2: Neuroanatomy

Although you have already been exposed to some neuroanatomy, it is now time to begin a more formal and detailed study of the area. Of the many introductory neuroanatomy books I read, most were good, but one stood out as especially understandable to me. Of the many brain atlases I have examined, this one was especially useful. I suggest these books, although other introductory ones may serve the purpose.

7. Chaplin, J. P., & Demers, A. (1978). *Primer of neurology and neurophysiology.* Melbourne: R. E. Krieger.
8. DeArmond, S. J., Fusco, M. M., & Dewey, M. M. (1989). *Structure*

of the human brain. A photographic atlas (3rd ed.). New York: Oxford University Press.

Level 3: Becoming More Sophisticated

The books at this level are getting more sophisticated but still remain readable without detailed knowledge of the brain. Both, as you will note, are by Luria. He wrote very well, and he wrote a number of classics on the topic of brain function.

9. Luria, A. R. (1966). *Higher cortical functions in man*. New York: Basic Books.
10. Luria, A. R. (1973). *The working brain. An introduction to neuropsychology*. New York: Basic Books.

Level 4: Neuropsychology and Neurology

By this time you are ready for the more sophisticated texts. Here are some of the best of them.

11. Bigler, E. D. (1988). *Diagnostic clinical neuropsychology* (rev. ed.). Austin: University of Texas Press.
12. Filskov, S. B., & Boll, T. J. (Eds.). (1981). *Handbook of clinical neuropsychology*. New York: Wiley.
13. Filskov, S. B., & Boll, T. J. (Eds.). (1986). *Handbook of clinical neuropsychology* (Vol. 2). New York: Wiley.
14. Golden, C. J. (1981). *Diagnosis and rehabilitation in clinical neuropsychology* (2nd ed.). Springfield: Charles C. Thomas.
15. Kolb, B., & Whishaw, I. Q. (1990). *Fundamentals of human neuropsychology* (3rd ed.). New York: W. H. Freeman.
16. Pincus, J., & Tucker, G. (1985). *Behavioral neurology* (3rd ed.). New York: Oxford Univeristy Press.
17. Lezak, M. (1983). *Neuropsychological assessment* (2nd ed.). New York: Oxford University Press.
18. Adams, R. D., & Victor, M. (1985). *Principles of neurology* (3rd ed.). New York: McGraw-Hill. (Although this is a neurology textbook, by this time in your reading program, much of it will be relatively understandable. I strongly suggest having a neurol-

ogy text readily available to you, if for no reason other than as a reference.)

19. Without listing them again, I refer you back to the end of Chapter 2 where a number of books were presented. Those books deal specifically with the interaction between organic diseases and psychiatric symptoms.

REFERENCES

Abrams, R., & Taylor, M. A. (1976). Catatonia: A prospective clinical study. *Archives of General Psychiatry, 33,* 579–581.

Adams, H. P., Jr., Jergenson, D. D., Kassell, N. F., & Sahs, A. L. (1980). Pitfalls in the recognition of subarachnoid hemorrhage. *Journal of the American Medical Association, 244,* 794–796.

Adams, H. P., Jr., Kassell, N. F., Boarini, D. J., & Kongable, G. (1991). The clinical spectrum of aneurysmal subarachnoid hemorrhage. *Journal of Stroke and Cerebrovascular Disease, 1,* 3–8.

Adams, R. D., & Victor, M. (1985). *Principles of neurology* (3rd ed.). New York: McGraw-Hill.

Alpers, B. J. (1940). Personality and emotional disorders associated with hypothalamic lesions. *Association for Research in Nervous and Mental Disease Proceedings, 20,* 725–748.

Anderson, A. (1982, July). Neurotoxic follies. *Psychology Today,* pp. 30–42.

Army Individual Test Battery. (1944). *Manual for directions and scoring.* Washington, DC: War Department, Adjutant General's Office.

Avery, T. L. (1971). Seven cases of frontal tumors with psychiatric presentation. *British Journal of Psychiatry, 119,* 19–23.

Barnes, R. F., Mason, J. C., Greer, C., & Ray, F. T. (1983). Medical illness in chronic psychiatric outpatients. *General Hospital Psychiatry, 5,* 191–195.

Barrett, E. T., Wheatley, R. D., & LaPlant, R. J. (1982). A brief clinical neuropsychologic screening battery: Statistical classification trials. *Journal of Clinical Psychology, 38,* 375–377.

Bartlett, J. E. A. (1957). Chronic psychosis following epilepsy. *American Journal of Psychiatry, 114,* 338–343.

Begali, V. (1987). *Head injury in children and adolescents. A resource and review for school and allied professionals.* Brandon, VT: Clinical Psychology Publishing Company.

Bender, L. A. (1938). A visual motor gestalt test and its clinical use. *American Orthopsychiatric Association Research Monographs,* No. 3.

Benson, D. F. (1973). Psychiatric aspects of aphasia. *British Journal of Psychiatry, 123,* 555–556.

Benson, D. F., & Blumer, D. (Eds.). (1975). *Psychiatric aspects of neurological disease.* New York: Grune & Stratton.

Benson, D. F., & Geschwind, N. (1975). Psychiatric conditions associated with focal lesions of the central nervous system. *American Handbook of Psychiatry, 4,* 208–243.

Benton, A. L. (1974). *Revised Visual Retention Test* (4th. ed.). New York: The Psychological Corporation.

Berg, R., Franzen, M., & Wedding, D. (1987). *Screening for brain impairment: A manual for mental health practice.* New York: Springer.

Bigler, E. D. (1988). *Diagnostic clinical neuropsychology* (rev. ed.). Austin: University of Texas Press.

Bingley, T. (1958). *Mental symptoms in temporal lobe epilepsy and temporal lobe gliomas.* Stockholm: Kobenhaven.

Bloom, F. E., & Lazerson, A. (1988). *Brain, mind, and behavior* (2nd ed.). New York: W.H. Freeman.

Braceland, F. J., & Griffin, M. E. (1950). Mental changes associated with multiple sclerosis (an interim report). *Association for Research in Nervous and Mental Disease Proceedings, 28,* 450.

Brenner, C., Friedman, A. P., & Merritt, H. H. (1947). Psychiatric syndromes in patients with organic brain disease: Diseases of the basal ganglia. *American Journal of Psychiatry, 103,* 733.

Brink, J. D., Garrett, A. L., Hale, W. R., Woo-Sam, J., & Nickel, V. C. (1970). Recovery of motor and intellectual function in children sustaining severe injuries. *Developmental Medicine and Child Neurology, 12,* 565–571.

Brown, G., Chadwick, O., Shaffer, D., Rutter, M., & Traub, M. (1981). A prospective study of children with head injuries: III. Psychiatric sequelae. *Psychological Medicine, 11,* 63–78.

Browning, C. H., Miller, S. I., & Tyson, R. L. (1974). The psychiatric emergency: A high risk medical patient. *Comprehensive Psychiatry, 15,* 153.

Burke, A. W. (1978). Physical disorder among day hospital patients. *British Journal of Psychiatry, 133,* 22–27.

Burton, L. (1968). *Vulnerable children.* New York: Schocken Books.

Canter, A. (1966). A background interference procedure to increase sensitivity of the Bender-Gestalt Test to organic brain damage. *Journal of Consulting Psychology, 30,* 91–95.

Carethers, M. (1988). Diagnosing vitamin B 12 deficiency, a common geriatric disorder. *Geriatrics, 43,* 89–112.

Carlson, R. J., Nayar, N., & Suh, M. (1981). Physical disorders among emergency psychiatric patients. *Canadian Journal of Psychiatry, 26,* 65–67.

Carlsson, G. S. (1986). Head injuries in a population study. *Acta Neurochirugia, 36,* 13–15.

Chaplin, J. P., & Demers, A. (1978). *Primer of neurology and neurophysiology.* Melbourne: R.E. Krieger.

Cole, G. (1978). Intracranial space-occupying masses in mental hospital patients: Necropsy study. *Journal of Neurological and Neurosurgical Psychiatry, 41,* 703.

Comroe, B. I. (1936). Follow-up study of 100 patients diagnosed as "neurosis." *Journal of Nervous and Mental Disease, 83,* 679–684.

Cummings, J. L. (1988). Organic psychosis. *Psychosomatics, 29,* 16–26.

DeArmond, S. J., Fusco, M. M., & Dewey, M. M. (1989). *Structure of the human brain. A photographic atlas* (3rd ed.). New York: Oxford University Press.

Department of Health, Education and Welfare. (1973). *Statistical Note 68.* Washington, DC: Author.

Direkze, M., Bayliss, S. B., & Cutting, J. C. (1971). Primary tumours of the frontal lobe. *British Journal of Clinical Practice, 25,* 207–213.

Eastwood, M. E. (1975). *The relation between physical and mental illness.* Toronto: University of Toronto Press.

Eastwood, M. E., Mindham, R. S., & Tennett, T. G. (1970). The physical status of psychiatric emergencies. *British Journal of Psychiatry, 116,* 545–550.

Eastwood, M. R., & Trevelyan, M. H. (1972). Relationship between physical and psychiatric disorder. *Psychological Medicine, 2,* 363–372.

Eilenberg, M. D., & Whatmore, M. B. (1961). Physical disease and psychiatric emergencies. *Comprehensive Psychiatry, 2,* 358–363.

Erickson, R. C., Calsyn, D. A., & Sheupach, C. S. (1978). Abbreviating the Halstead-Reitan neuropsychological test battery. *Journal of Clinical Psychology, 34,* 922–926.

Ervin, F., Epstein, A. A., & King, H. E. (1955). Behavior of epileptic and non-epileptic patients with temporal spikes. *Archives of Neurology and Psychiatry, 74,* 488–496.

Faust, C. (1966). Different psychological consequences due to superior frontal and orbital-basal lesions. *International Journal of Neurology, 5,* 410–421.

Filskov, S. B. (1984). Neuropsychological screening. In T. A. Keller & L. G. Ritt (Eds.), *Innovations in clinical practice: A source book* (Vol. 2, pp. 17–25). Sarasota: Professional Resource Exchange.

Filskov, S. B., & Boll, T. J. (Eds.). (1981). *Handbook of clinical neuropsychology.* New York: Wiley.

Filskov, S. B., & Boll, T. J. (Eds.). (1986). *Handbook of clinical neuropsychology* (Vol. 2). New York: Wiley.

Forsythe, R. J., Ilk, C. R., Bard, J., & Wolford, J. A. (1977). Primary medical care in psychiatry. *Current Psychiatric Therapy, 17,* 91–97.

Franzen, M., & Berg, R. (1989). *Screening children for brain impairment.* New York: Springer.

Gardner, H. (1974). *The shattered mind.* New York: Knopf.

Gelenberg, A. J. (1976). The catatonic syndrome. *Lancet, 1,* 1339–1341.

Gibbs, F. A. (1951). Ictal and non-ictal psychiatric disorders in temporal lobe epilepsy. *Journal of Nervous and Mental Disease, 113,* 522–528.

Golden, C. J. (1981). *Diagnosis and rehabilitation in clinical neuropsychology* (2nd ed.). Springfield: Charles C. Thomas.

Golden, C. J. (1987). *Luria-Nebraska Neuropsychological Battery: Children's Revision.* Los Angeles: Western Psychological Services.

Golden, C. J., Hammeke, T. A., & Purisch, A. D. (1980). *Manual for the Luria-Nebraska Neuropsychological Battery.* Los Angeles: Western Psychological Services.

Goldstein, G., & Neuringer, C. (1966). Schizophrenic and organic signs on the Trail Making Test. *Perceptual and Motor Skills, 22,* 347.

Gordon, N. G. (1972). The Trail Making Test in neuropsychological diagnosis. *Journal of Clinical Psychology, 28,* 167–169.

Gordon, N.G. (1978). Diagnostic efficiency of the Trail Making Test as a function of cutoff score, diagnosis and age. *Perceptual and Motor Skills, 47,* 191–195.

Graham, F. K., & Kendall, B. S. (1960). Memory-For-Designs Test: Revised general manual. *Perceptual and Motor Skills, 11,* Monograph Supplement 2-VII, 147–188.

Hall, R. C., Gardner, E. R., Stickney, S. K., LeCann, A. F., & Popkin, M. K. (1980). Physical illness manifesting as psychiatric disease. II. Analysis of a state hospital inpatient population. *Archives of General Psychiatry, 37,* 989–995.

Hall, R. C., Gruzenski, W. P., & Popkin, M. K. (1979). Differential diagnosis of somatopsychic disorders. *Psychosomatics, 20,* 381–389.

Hall, R. C., & Popkin, M. K. (1977). Psychological symptoms of physical origin. *The Female Patient, 2,* 43–47.

Hall, R. C., Popkin, M. K., DeVaul, R. A., Faillace, L. A., & Stickney, S. K. (1978). Physical illness presenting as psychiatric disease. *Archives of General Psychiatry, 35,* 1315–1320.

Halstead, W. C., & Wepman, J. M. (1959). The Halstead-Wepman aphasia screening test. *Journal of Speech and Hearing Disorders, 14,* 9–15.

Hartlage, L. C. (1984). Neuropsychological screening of children. In T. A. Keller & L. G. Ritt (Eds.), *Innovations in clinical practice: A source book* (Vol. 3, pp. 153–164). Sarasota: Professional Resource Exchange.

Hebb, D. O. (1949). *The organization of behavior.* New York: Wiley.

Herridge, C. F. (1960). Physical disorders in psychiatric illness. A study of 209 consecutive admissions. *Lancet, 2,* 949–951.

Hertzig, M. E., & Birch, H. G. (1968). Neurological organization in psychiatrically disturbed adolescents. *Archives of General Psychiatry, 19,* 528–537.

Holmes, C. B. (1988). *The head-injured college student.* Springfield: Charles C. Thomas.

Hunter, R., Blackwood, W., & Bull, J. (1968). Three cases of frontal meningioma presenting psychiatrically. *British Medical Journal, 3,* 9–16.

Hynd, G. W., & Obrzut, J. E. (1981). *Neuropsychological assessment and the school age child.* New York: Grune & Stratton.

Hynd, G. W., & Semrud-Clikeman, M. (1989). Dyslexia and brain morphology. *Psychological Bulletin, 106,* 447–482.

Illowsky, B., & Kirch, D. (1988). Polydipsia and hyponatremia in psychiatric patients. *American Journal of Psychiatry, 145,* 675–683.

Jefferson, J. W., & Marshall, J. R. (1981). *Neuropsychiatric features of medical disorders.* New York: Plenum.

Johnson, D. A. W. (1968). The evaluation of routine physical examination in psychiatric cases. *Practitioner, 200,* 686–691.

Kanakaratnam, G., & Direkze, M. (1976). Aspects of primary tumours of the frontal lobe. *British Journal of Clinical Practice, 30,* 220–221.

Katz, E. R., Dolgin, M. J., & Varni, J. W. (1990). Cancer in children and adolescents. In A. M. Gross & R. S. Drabman (Eds.), *Handbook of clinical behavioral pediatrics* (pp. 129–146). New York: Plenum.

Kellner, R. (1966). Psychiatric ill health following physical illness. *British Journal of Psychiatry, 112,* 71–73.

Keschner, M., Bender, M. B., & Strauss, I. (1936). Mental symptoms in cases of tumor of the temporal lobe. *Archives of Neurology and Psychiatry, 35,* 572–596.

Keschner, M., Bender, M. B., & Strauss, I. (1937). Mental symptoms in cases of subtentorial tumor. *Archives of Neurology and Psychiatry, 37,* 1–15.

Klawans, H. L., Moskovitz, C., Nauseida, P. A., & Weiner, W. J. (1979). Levodopa-induced dopaminergic hypersensitivity in the pathogenesis of psychiatric and neurologic disorders. *International Journal of Neurology, 13,* 225–235.

Klonoff, H., & Low, M. (1974). Disordered brain function in young children and early adolescents: Neuropsychological and electroencephalographic correlates. In R. M. Reitan & L. A. Davidson (Eds.), *Clinical neuropsychology: Current status and applications* (pp. 121–178). New York: Wiley.

Kolb, B., & Whishaw, I. Q. (1990). *Fundamentals of human neuropsychology* (3rd ed.). New York: W. H. Freeman.

Kopp, C. B., & Kaler, S. R. (1989). Risk in infancy: Origins and implications. *American Psychologist, 44,* 224–230.

Koran, L. M., Sox, H. C., Marton, K. I., Moltzen, S., Sox, C. H., Kraemer, H. C., Imai, K., Kelsey, T. G., Rose, T. G., Levin, L. C., & Satish, C. (1989). Medical evaluation of psychiatric patients. *Archives of General Psychiatry, 46,* 733–740.

Koranyi, E. K. (1972). Physical health and illness in a psychiatric outpatient department population. *Canadian Psychiatric Association Journal, 17,* SS109-SS116.

Koranyi, E. K. (1977). Fatalities in 2,070 psychiatric outpatients. *Archives of General Psychiatry, 34,* 1137–1142.

Koranyi, E. K. (1979). Morbidity and rate of undiagnosed physical illness in a psychiatric clinic population. *Archives of General Psychiatry, 36,* 414–419.

Lawall, J. (1976). Psychiatric presentations of seizure disorders. *American Journal of Psychiatry, 133,* 321–323.

Lezak, M. D. (1983). *Neuropsychological assessment* (2nd ed.). New York: Oxford University Press.

Lipowski, Z. J. (1975). Psychiatry of somatic diseases: Epidemiology, pathogenesis, classification. *Comprehensive Psychiatry, 16,* 105–124.

Lishman, W. (1978). *Organic psychiatry: The psychological consequences of cerebral disorder.* Oxford: Blackwell Scientific.

Lovett Doust, J. W. (1952). Psychiatric aspects of somatic immunity. Differential incidence of physical disease in the histories of psychiatric patients. *British Journal of Social Medicine, 6,* 49–67.

Lubin, B., Larsen, R. M., Matarazzo, J. D., & Seever, M. (1985). Psychological test usage patterns in five professional settings. *American Psychologist, 40,* 857–861.

Luria, A. R. (1966). *Higher cortical functions in man.* New York: Basic Books.

Luria, A. R. (1968). *The mind of a mnemonist.* New York: Basic Books.

Luria, A. R. (1972). *The man with a shattered world.* New York: Basic Books.

Luria, A. R. (1973). *The working brain. An introduction to neuropsychology.* New York: Basic Books.

Maguire, G. P., & Granville-Grossman, K. L. (1968). Physical illness in psychiatric patients. *British Journal of Psychiatry, 115,* 1365–1369.

Malamud, N. (1957). Psychiatric symptoms and the limbic lobe. *Bulletin of the Los Angeles Neurological Society, 22,* 131–139.

Malamud, N. (1966). The epileptogenic focus in temporal lobe epilepsy from a pathological standpoint. *Archives of Neurology, 14,* 190–195.

Malamud, N. (1967). Psychiatric disorder with intracranial tumors of the limbic system. *Archives of Neurology, 17,* 113–123.

Mannino, F., & Wylie, H. (1965). Evaluation of the physical examination as part of a psychiatric clinic intake practice. *American Journal of Psychiatry, 122,* 175–179.

Mark, S., & Gath, A. (1978). *Psychological disorders of children.* Baltimore: Williams and Wilkins.

Marshall, H. E. S. (1949). Incidence of physical disorders among psychiatric inpatients. *British Medical Journal, 2,* 468–470.

Martin, E. A. (1962). Organic disease as the cause of admission to a psychiatric hospital. *Journal of the Irish Medical Association, 50,* 117–122.

McIntyre, J. S., & Romano, J. (1977). Is there a stethoscope in the house (and is it used)? *Archives of General Psychiatry, 34,* 1147–1151.

Meyer, B. C. (1958). Some psychiatric aspects of surgical practice. *Psychosomatic Medicine, 20,* 203–214.

Mezzich, J. E., & Moses, J. A. (1980). Efficient screening for brain dysfunction. *Biological Psychiatry, 15,* 333–337.

Moss, R., D'Amico, S., & Maletta, G. (1987). Mental dysfunction as a sign of organic illness in the elderly. *Geriatrics, 42,* 35–40.

Muecke, L. N., & Krueger, D. W. (1981). Physical findings in a psychiatric clinic population. *American Journal of Psychiatry, 138,* 1241–1242.

Mulder, D. W., & Daly, D. (1952). Psychiatric symptoms associated with lesions of the temporal lobe. *Journal of the American Medical Association, 150,* 173–176.

National Institute of Neurological Disorders and Stroke. (1989). *Interagency head injury task force report.* Bethesda: National Institutes of Health.

Ornstein, R., & Thompson, R. F. (1984). *The amazing brain.* Boston: Houghton Mifflin.

Patton, R. B., & Sheppard, J. A. (1956). Intracranial tumors found at autopsy in mental patients. *American Journal of Psychiatry, 113,* 319–324.

Phillips, R. J. (1937). Physical disorder in 164 consecutive admissions to a mental hospital: The incidence and signficance. *British Medical Journal, 11,* 363.

Pincus, J., & Tucker, G. (1985). *Behavioral neurology* (3rd ed.). New York: Oxford University Press.

Pless, I. B., & Roghman, K. J. (1971). Chronic illness and its consequences: Observations based on three epidemiological surveys. *Journal of Pediatrics, 79,* 351.

Plum, F., & Posner, J. B. (1982). *The diagnosis of stupor and coma* (3rd ed.). Philadelphia: F. A. Davis.

Reitan, R. M. (1984). *Aphasia and sensory-perceptual deficits in adults.* Tucson: Neuropsychology Press.

Reitan, R. M., & Davison, L. A. (1974). *Clinical neuropsychology: Current status and applications.* New York: Hemisphere.

Remington, F. B., & Rubert, S. L. (1962). Why patients with brain tumors come to psychiatric hospitals. *American Journal of Psychiatry, 119,* 256–257.

Rimel, R., Giordini, B., Barth, J. T., Boll, T. J., & Jane, J. A. (1981). Disability caused by minor head injury. *Neurosurgery, 9,* 221–228.

Ritvo, E. R., Ornitz, E. M., & Walter, R. D. (1970). Correlation of psychiatric diagnosis and EEG findings: A double-blind study of 184 hospitalized children. *American Journal of Psychiatry, 126,* 988–996.

Roberts, J. K. A. (1984). *Differential diagnosis in neuropsychiatry*. Chichester: Wiley.

Rodin, E. A., DeJong, R. N., Waggoner, R. W., & Bagchi, B. K. (1957). Relationship between certain forms of psychomotor epilepsy and "schizophrenia": I. Diagnostic considerations. *Archives of Neurology and Psychiatry, 77*, 449–463.

Roessler, R., & Greenfield, N. S. (1961). Incidence of somatic disease in psychiatric patients. *Psychosomatic Medicine, 23*, 413–419.

Romano, J. (1970). The elimination of the internship: An act of regression. *American Journal of Psychiatry, 126*, 1565–1576.

Rossman, P. L. (1969). Organic diseases resembling functional disorders. *Hospital Medicine, 5*, 72–76.

Rutter, M. (1977). Brain damage syndromes in childhood: Concepts and findings. *Journal of Child Psychology and Psychiatry, 18*, 1–21.

Rutter, M. (1981). Psychological sequelae of brain damage in children. *American Journal of Psychiatry, 138*, 1533–1544.

Rutter, M., Graham, P., & Yule, W. (1970). *A neuropsychiatric study in childhood*. London: Heinemann Medical.

Sacks, O. (1985). *The man who mistook his wife for a hat and other clinical tales*. New York: Harper & Row.

Sandifer, M. G. (1977). The education of the psychiatrist as a physician. *American Journal of Psychiatry, 134*, 50–53.

Saravay, S., & Koran, L. (1977) Organic disease mistakenly diagnosed as psychiatric. *Psychosomatics, 18*, 6–11.

Seidel, V. P., Chadwick, O., & Rutter, M. (1975). Psychological disorders in crippled children: A comparative study of children with and without brain damage. *Developmental Medicine and Child Neurology, 17*, 563–573.

Seidman, L. J. (1983). Schizophrenia and brain dysfunction: An integration of recent neurodiagnostic findings. *Psychological Bulletin, 94*, 195–238.

Selecki, B. R. (1965). Intracranial space-occupying lesions among patients admitted to mental hospitals. *Medical Journal of Australia, 1*, 383–390.

Selzer, B., & Sherwin, I. (1978). Organic brain syndrome: An empirical study and critical review. *American Journal of Psychiatry, 135*, 13–21.

Serafetinides, E. A., & Falconer, M. A. (1962). The effects of temporal lobectomy in epileptic patients with psychosis. *Journal of Mental Science, 108*, 584–593.

Shaffer, D., Chadwick, O., & Rutter, M. (1975). Psychiatric outcome of localized head injury in children. *CIBA Foundation Symposium, 34* (new series).

Shulman, R. (1977). Psychogenic illness with physical manifestations and the other side of the coin. *Lancet, 1*, 524–526.

Slater, E. (1965). Diagnosis of hysteria. *British Medical Journal, 1*, 1395–1399.

Slater, E., & Beard, A. W. (1963). The schizophrenia-like psychoses of epilepsy. *British Journal of Psychiatry, 109*, 95–150.

Slater, E., & Glithero, E. (1965). A follow-up of patients diagnosed as suffering from "hysteria." *Journal of Psychosomatic Research, 9,* 9–13.

Smith, T. E., & Boyce, E. M. (1962). The relationship of the Trail Making Test to psychiatric symptomatology. *Journal of Clinical Psychology, 18,* 450–454.

Snaith, R. P., & Jacobson, S. (1965). The observation ward and the psychiatric emergency. *British Journal of Psychiatry, 111,* 18–26.

Soniat, T. L. L. (1951). Psychiatric symptoms associated with intracranial neoplasms. *American Journal of Psychiatry, 108,* 19–22.

Spudis, E., Rogers, J., & Stein, L. (1977). The psychiatrist's management of patients with undiagnosed brain neoplasm. *Southern Medical Journal, 70,* 405.

Stokes, J. F., Nabarro, J. D. N., Rosenheim, M. L., & Dunkley, E. W. (1954). Physical disease in a mental observation unit. *Lancet, 2,* 862–863.

Strauss, I., & Keschner, M. (1935). Mental symptoms in cases of tumor of the frontal lobes. *Archives of Neurology and Psychiatry, 33,* 986–1005.

Strub, R. L., & Black, F. W. (1985). *The mental status examination in neurology* (2nd. ed.). Philadelphia: F. A. Davis.

Strub, R. L., & Black, F. W. (1988). *Neurobehavioral disorders: A clinical approach.* Philadelphia: F. A. Davis.

Stuteville, P., & Welch, K. (1958). Subdural hematoma in the elderly. *Journal of the American Medical Association, 168,* 1445–1449.

Taylor, R. L. (1990). *Distinguishing psychological from organic disorders. Screening for psychological masquerade.* New York: Springer.

Tissenbaum, M., Harter, H., & Friedman, A. (1951). Organic neurological syndrome diagnosed as functional disorders. *Journal of the American Medical Association, 147,* 1519–1521.

Tramontana, M. G., Sherrets, S. D., & Golden, C. J. (1980). Brain dysfunction in youngsters with psychiatric disorders: Application of Selz-Reitan rules for neuropsychological diagnosis. *Clinical Neuropsychology, 2,* 118–123.

Tupper, D. E. (1986). Neuropsychological screening and soft signs. In J. E. Obrzut & G. W. Hynd (Eds.), *Child neuropsychology* (Vol 2, pp. 139–186). San Diego: Academic Press.

Vieweg, W. V. R., David, J. J., Rowe, W. T., Wampler, G. J., Burns, W. J., & Spradlin, W. W. (1985). Death from self-induced water intoxication among patients with schizophrenic disorders. *Journal of Nervous and Mental Disease, 173,* 161–165.

Watson, C. G., & Buranen, C. (1979). The frequency and identification of false positive conversion reactions. *Journal of Nervous and Mental Disease, 167,* 243–247.

Watson, C. G., Thomas, R. W., Anderson, D., & Felling, J. (1968). Differentiation of organics from schizophrenics at two chronicity levels by use of the Reitan-Halstead organic test battery. *Journal of Consulting and Clinical Psychology, 32,* 679–684.

Wechsler, D. (1945). A standardized memory scale for clinical use. *Journal of Psychology, 19,* 87–95.

Wechsler, D. (1974). *Wechsler Intelligence Scale for Children—Revised.* New York: The Psychological Corporation.

Wechsler, D. (1981). *Wechsler Adult Intelligence Scale—Revised.* New York: The Psychological Corporation.

Wechsler, D. (1987). *Wechsler Memory Scale—Revised.* San Antonio: The Psychological Corporation.

Weinberger, D. R. (1984). Brain disease and psychiatric illness: When should a psychiatrist order a CAT scan? *American Journal of Psychiatry, 141,* 1521–1527.

Wells, C. E., & Duncan, G. W. (Eds.). (1980). *Neurology for psychiatrists.* Philadelphia: F. A. Davis.

Whitlock, F. A. (1967). The aetiology of hysteria. *Acta Psychiatrica Scandinavica, 43,* 144–162.

Whitlock, F. A., & Price, J. (1974). Use of beta-adrenergic receptor blocking drugs in psychiatry. *Drugs, 8,* 109–124.

Wicks-Nelson, R., & Israel, A. C. (1991). *Behavior disorders of childhood* (2nd ed.). Englewood Cliffs: Prentice-Hall.

Williamson, J., Stokoe, I. H., Gray, S., Fisher, M., Smith, A., McGhee, A., & Stephenson, E. (1964). Old people at home. Their unreported needs. *Lancet, 1,* 1117–1120.

Wingfield, R. T. (1967). Psychiatric symptoms that signal organic disease. *Virginia Medical Monthly, 94,* 153–157.

Wood, M. W., White, R. J., & Kernohan, J. W. (1957). One hundred intracranial meningiomas found incidentally at necropsy. *Journal of Neuropathology and Experimental Neurology, 16,* 337–340.

Wynne-Davis, D. W. (1965). Physical illness in psychiatric out-patients. *British Journal of Psychiatry, 111,* 27–33.

INDEX